CAMBRIDGE LIBP '

Books of enduri.

Archaeo

The discovery of material remains from th _____ ancient past has always been a source of fascination, but the _.ciopment of archaeology as an academic discipline which interpreted such finds is relatively recent. It was the work of Winckelmann at Pompeii in the 1760s which first revealed the potential of systematic excavation to scholars and the wider public. Pioneering figures of the nineteenth century such as Schliemann, Layard and Petrie transformed archaeology from a search for ancient artifacts, by means as crude as using gunpowder to break into a tomb, to a science which drew from a wide range of disciplines - ancient languages and literature, geology, chemistry, social history - to increase our understanding of human life and society in the remote past.

Travels in the Central Parts of Indo-China (Siam), Cambodia, and Laos

As a young man, French naturalist Henri Mouhot (1826–61) taught languages in Russia and travelled widely in Europe with his brother Charles, sketching people and landscapes, and taking photographs. The brothers both married descendants of the explorer Mungo Park (whose journals are also reissued). Not long afterwards, possibly inspired by Bowring's 1857 book on Siam (also reissued), Mouhot decided to explore South-East Asia. He travelled independently for three years in Thailand, Cambodia and Laos, where he eventually died of a fever. This engaging two-volume account of his experiences was compiled by his brother from his papers, and published in 1864 with many illustrations based on Mouhot's sketches. Volume 1 focuses mainly on Thailand and Cambodia, where Mouhot met several kings, travelled by elephant through difficult terrain, and visited the ruins of Ayuthia and Angkor. Mouhot's enthusiasm for the region's wildlife, landscapes and people rarely wavers, despite the challenging conditions.

Cambridge University Press has long been a pioneer in the reissuing of out-of-print titles from its own backlist, producing digital reprints of books that are still sought after by scholars and students but could not be reprinted economically using traditional technology. The Cambridge Library Collection extends this activity to a wider range of books which are still of importance to researchers and professionals, either for the source material they contain, or as landmarks in the history of their academic discipline.

Drawing from the world-renowned collections in the Cambridge University Library and other partner libraries, and guided by the advice of experts in each subject area, Cambridge University Press is using state-of-the-art scanning machines in its own Printing House to capture the content of each book selected for inclusion. The files are processed to give a consistently clear, crisp image, and the books finished to the high quality standard for which the Press is recognised around the world. The latest print-on-demand technology ensures that the books will remain available indefinitely, and that orders for single or multiple copies can quickly be supplied.

The Cambridge Library Collection brings back to life books of enduring scholarly value (including out-of-copyright works originally issued by other publishers) across a wide range of disciplines in the humanities and social sciences and in science and technology.

Travels in the Central Parts of Indo-China (Siam), Cambodia, and Laos

During the Years 1858, 1859, and 1860

VOLUME 1

HENRI MOUHOT
EDITED AND TRANSLATED BY
CHARLES MOUHOT

CAMBRIDGE
UNIVERSITY PRESS

CAMBRIDGE
UNIVERSITY PRESS

University Printing House, Cambridge, CB2 8BS, United Kingdom

Cambridge University Press is part of the University of Cambridge.

It furthers the University's mission by disseminating knowledge in the pursuit of education, learning and research at the highest international levels of excellence.

www.cambridge.org
Information on this title: www.cambridge.org/9781108084086

© in this compilation Cambridge University Press 2015

This edition first published 1864
This digitally printed version 2015

ISBN 978-1-108-08408-6 Paperback

This book reproduces the text of the original edition. The content and language reflect the beliefs, practices and terminology of their time, and have not been updated.

Cambridge University Press wishes to make clear that the book, unless originally published by Cambridge, is not being republished by, in association or collaboration with, or with the endorsement or approval of, the original publisher or its successors in title.

The original edition of this book contains a number of oversize plates which it has not been possible to reproduce to scale in this edition. They can be found online at www.cambridge.org/9781108084086

TRAVELS

IN THE

CENTRAL PARTS OF INDO-CHINA

(SIAM),

CAMBODIA, AND LAOS.

Drawn by M. Bocourt, from a Photograph.

THE KING AND QUEEN OF SIAM.

TRAVELS

CENTRAL PARTS OF INDO-CHINA

(SIAM),

CAMBODIA, AND LAOS,

DURING THE YEARS 1858, 1859, AND 1860.

BY THE LATE

M. HENRI MOUHOT,

FRENCH NATURALIST.

IN TWO VOLUMES.—Vol. I.

WITH ILLUSTRATIONS.

LONDON:

JOHN MURRAY, ALBEMARLE STREET,

1864.

LONDON: PRINTED BY WILLIAM CLOWES AND SONS, STAMFORD STREET, AND CHARING CROSS.

DEDICATION.

TO THE LEARNED SOCIETIES OF ENGLAND, WHO HAVE
FAVOURED WITH THEIR ENCOURAGEMENT THE
JOURNEY OF M. HENRI MOUHOT TO THE REMOTE
LANDS OF SIAM, LAOS, AND CAMBODIA.

I TRUST that the members of those scientific societies who kindly
supported and encouraged my brother in his travels and labours,
will receive favourably the documents collected by the family of
the intrepid traveller, whom death carried off in the flower of his
age, in the midst of his discoveries.

Had he been able to accomplish fully the end at which he
aimed, it would certainly have been to you that he would have
offered the fruits of his travels : he would have felt it his first
duty to testify his gratitude and esteem to the worthy repre-
sentatives of science in that great, free, and generous English
nation who adopted him. Half English by his marriage, M.
Mouhot still preserved his love for his own country : there,
however, for various reasons he did not receive the encouragement he anticipated, and it was on the hospitable soil of England
that he met with that aid and support, which not only her
scientific men, but the whole nation, delight in affording to
explorations in unknown countries, ever attended by perils and
hardships. The journal of the unfortunate traveller shows his
feelings of affection for the two countries which he loved
equally, and his devotion to science, art, and the progress of
civilization.

I therefore feel it an imperative duty to express to you and to

the whole English nation the sentiments of gratitude to which
this good and loyal Frenchman so often gave utterance, while
engaged in the work to which he spontaneously devoted
himself, and in which he was sustained by your counsels and
assistance.

Receive therefore from Madame Mouhot and myself, as a
legacy left by her dear husband and my affectionate brother,
the expression of our gratitude; and accept the work, left
imperfect, it is true, but which we hope will prove how much
has been lost by the death of a brave man, who, allied to the
family of Mungo Park, met the same fate in the East that
that illustrious explorer did in Africa.   M. Mouhot's premature
end did not permit him to correct and arrange his journal,
which is an additional reason for claiming indulgence from
you, whose enlightened minds and generous benevolence will
know how to appreciate the circumstances under which this
posthumous work sees the light.

CHARLES MOUHOT.

Jersey, 1st December, 1862.

Drawn by M. Bocourt, from a Photograph.

ONE OF THE SONS OF THE KING OF SIAM.

PREFACE.

As will be seen, this work is compiled from the
private letters of M. Mouhot to his family and
friends, and from his journal. I had also the
benefit of the paper destined by my brother for
the Archæological Society of London, on the interesting ruins of Ongcor. Among the documents
which, thanks to the active kindness of Sir R.
Schomburgh, British Consul at Bangkok, of Dr.
Campbell, R.N., and of M. D'Istria, French Consul,
reached me as early as possible after my brother's
death, I found valuable sketches and drawings,
together with various unfinished papers relative to
his different scientific researches in the countries
he had visited and in districts which had only
recently been brought into notice by the advance

of commerce, and by the military expeditions which had been sent to the extreme East.

The family of M. Mouhot were divided in opinion as to the course to be adopted with regard to these varied materials. Should they be kept in a portfolio as a sacred but barren deposit, or should they be arranged in the best manner possible and laid before the public?

After grave consideration they yielded to the representations of friends of the deceased, and to myself was confided the painful but interesting task of superintending the arrangement of the notes, sketches, and documents for publication. I accordingly set about it at once, under the first impressions of grief at the loss I had sustained, and guided only by fraternal love, for I lay no claim to the title of author. I have simply classified the masses of papers, the fruit of four years' travel, and added a few explanatory notes.

I have already stated the motives which induced me to dedicate this work to the Savans of England, more especially to those with whom my brother was connected through science or literature.

Let me give a short sketch of the work for

which we claim the indulgence of the public. I
have first, preserving the chronological order,
divided the journal into chapters, inserting in
their appropriate places such portions of the private
letters as served to throw light on the subject.
This forms the body of the work.

In an Appendix I have inserted the Chinese
tales translated by the author during his residence in Siam—some unfinished papers which are
only specimens of a zoological work which my
brother intended to publish—the descriptions of
the principal entomological and conchological specimens discovered by him, and which are now
deposited in the Museums of London and Paris—
the Cambodian vocabulary, a proof of his industry,
of the variety of his knowledge, and of the care
with which he collected everything which might
be useful to his successors in the difficult path
which he opened to them.

Lastly, I have collected the letters of my brother
to his family and other correspondents, together
with some letters addressed to him, a few of which
were never even received, while others only reached

their destination after his death, or remained in the hands of friends who were charged to deliver them. This correspondence tends, I think, to display my brother's character, the delicacy of his mind, and the goodness of his heart, qualities which have been recognised by so many, both during his life and after his death.

The engravings from his drawings will impart interest to the descriptions of the ruins and vast buildings which he discovered in the interior of Siam and Cambodia, testifying to an advanced state of civilization in former times, and which, I venture to think, deserve to be brought into notice. They will also familiarize the reader with the manners, customs, and appearance of the country. My aim has been to be useful to those who deign to read these pages ; and, if fidelity be merit in a book, I trust the reader will be satisfied.

Even should there be any errors in the numbers of the population, and similar details concerning the little-known countries which my brother traversed, I beg the reader to view them with indulgence, bearing in mind that most of this journal was written in pencil, sent home from a long distance, and some of it half effaced ;—illegible, indeed, to any one to whom his writing was not as well known as it was to Madame Mouhot and myself, and who were not as intimate with the heart and thoughts of the writer.

All these reasons induce me to reckon on the indulgence of the public.

The Memoir which follows was written by a friend in Holland. The historical notice which I have thus introduced, appeared to me useful, in order to give a clearer idea of the country which my brother has contributed to make better known, and where he sealed with his death his devotion to travel and scientific pursuits.

Let me add, in conclusion, that the family of M. Mouhot gladly embrace the opportunity of thanking publicly all those who have given aid to the traveller, and have testified their friendship for him; several are mentioned in the course of the book by my brother himself, but others, from whom he received equal kindness and support before embarking on his perilous journey into unknown regions, have not perhaps been noticed as they deserved. It was neither forgetfulness nor ingratitude on his part; his death is his excuse.

CHARLES MOUHOT.

Adelaide Lodge, Jersey,
January, 1863.

so much in its various parts; still he felt deeply the condition of the serfs, a condition which Alexander II., moved
by generous sentiments, wishes now to reform. This state
of things made a painful impression on the heart of the
young Frenchman, and on his return to his own country
he gave vent to his feelings in a book called 'Slavery in
Russia;' and in order to engage better the attention of
the reader he wove it into the form of a novel, in which
he was enabled to employ the resources of illustration,
and to depict the manners of the country. This work,
however, which touched on many of the leading questions
of the day, was never published, and is only mentioned
here as an illustration of his generous feelings.

The war which broke out in the East induced him to
leave Russia, although, doubtless, owing to his numerous
friends, he might safely have awaited there the return of
a time more propitious to the cultivation of art and science;
but his feelings as a Frenchman revolted from this, and
he also felt that the gravity of the events about to take
place would turn every mind from all but warlike
subjects.

M. Mouhot, therefore, returned to France to his father
and to a loved brother, who became the companion of his
new travels in Germany, Belgium, and the north of Italy;
and everywhere they laboured by means of photography
to make known the works of the great masters and the
beauties of the country, exercising their profession like
real artists. They afterwards resolved to visit Holland,
where photography was less widely known than in other

countries. After staying there some time they removed their establishment to England in 1856, the more willingly as they had both married English ladies, relatives of Mungo Park, and having friends willing to push on the two young men, who, full of energy, possessed the qualities necessary for success in an artistic or scientific career. During some ensuing years the two brothers pursued their calling together, and shared each other's pleasures and cares; but Henri afterwards found in a peaceful life at Jersey an opportunity of resuming his studies in Natural History, devoting himself particularly to Ornithology and Conchology. These studies revived in him the desire for foreign travel; and beautiful as was the island where he lived—and where his time was divided between his home, his books, and out-door pursuits—his thirst for knowledge made him long for a wider field of research, and one less explored by modern travellers. An English book on Siam came into his possession about this time, as though sent by the hand of destiny, and to visit that country became the object of his aspirations. The great Geographical and Zoological Societies of London, capable of appreciating the man of merit, approved of his project, and aided him efficaciously in its prosecution; and M. H. Mouhot quitted his wife, brother, and all his friends and every advantage of civilization, in order to visit, in the cause of science, regions little known, but where, through much fatigue and danger, the prospect of a glorious future opened itself before him.

He was already well prepared for the life; active, strong,

and blessed with an excellent constitution: his physical
strength was beyond the average—a result of the gym-
nastic sports in which he had taken pleasure in his youth,
and of his habitual sobriety.   He had never had an attack
of fever, nor any other illness; and he resisted for four
years the effects of a tropical climate, incredible fatigue,
bad food, and nights passed in forests, without any apparent
loss of health or strength, which is doubtless to be attributed to his never taking spirits, and wine only very
sparingly.

His intellectual and moral qualities did not seem less
to promise success; both a *savant* and an artist, he was
also an indefatigable hunter, and had a degree of kindness
mingled with his courage which was sure to gain the good-
will of the uncivilized people among whom he had to live.
In all these respects M. Mouhot fulfilled the expectations
of the *savans* of England and of his numerous friends, as
is evident by the rich collections made by him in so short
a time, by the cordial welcome which he met with throughout his travels, by the respect paid to him by all learned
men, and by the unanimous feelings of regret at his death,
both in England and on the Continent.   Although a Protestant, he inspired sincere friendships among the Catholic
missionaries in Siam and the other countries he visited
from 1858 to 1861, friendships which are clearly shown
in his journal and letters.

We shall not say much about his travels; they form the
subject of this work, which, even in its unfinished state,
we trust will present much important information to the

geographer and archæologist, to the naturalist and linguist.
Many capable of judging have already hastened to pay
their tribute of praise to the traveller who has enriched
such various branches of science, and displayed to the
world the riches of the extreme East.

M. Mouhot dedicated the last four years of his life to
exploring the interior of Siam; he first travelled through
that country, then through Cambodia, and afterwards re-
ascended the Mekong as far as the frontiers of Laos;
visited one of the savage and independent tribes inhabiting the district between those two countries and Cochin
China; then, after having crossed the great lake Touli-
Sap, he explored the provinces of Ongcor and Battambong,
where he discovered splendid ruins, especially the Temple
of Ongcor the Great, which is nearly perfect, and perhaps
unparalleled in the world.

Passing from the basin of the Mekong into that of the
Menam, he saw mountains of which the principal peak
was more than 6000 feet high.   He returned occasionally
to Bangkok, the capital of Siam, in order to make preparations for fresh expeditions.   The loss, ·by the wreck
of the *Sir James Brooke*, of a very valuable collection, did
not discourage him; but he set about at once to replace it.
At the time of his death, which happened on 10th November, 1861, he was *en route* for the provinces south-west
of China, when, having already penetrated far into the
interior, he was attacked by the jungle fever, and died
after twenty-two days' illness.   His energetic mind, full of
the task he had to perform, remained clear to the end,

and a few last words were written by him, his strength of will overcoming his weakness.

He set out for Louang-Prabang on 15th October, and on the 18th halted at H—— (the name is unfinished in the manuscript); the next day he felt the first symptoms of the fever to which he fell a victim. From the 29th October he wrote nothing. The last words in the journal, "Have pity on me, O my God," show the religious principles which had guided his life.

All that we know of his last days and his lamentable end, was learned from his two native servants, who were strongly attached to him; and through Sir R. Schomburgh, the English Consul at Bangkok, and Dr. Campbell, Surgeon R.N., who was attached to the British consulate, and who returned shortly afterwards to England, when he placed all the papers, notes, and drawings left by M. Mouhot in the hands of his widow and of M. Charles Mouhot, whose task it has been to arrange this legacy as methodically as possible, considering the great difficulty of finding the connecting links of his various descriptions.

The 'Athenæum' and the 'Illustrated London News'* both inserted an account of the death of M. H. Mouhot; and the latter journal justly designated his death as another addition to the long list of martyrs to science. It likewise gave a short sketch of the discoveries and scientific services of this intrepid traveller.

Ornithology, entomology, and other branches of natural

* Number for August 9, 1862, which also contained a tolerably good portrait of M. Mouhot.

history, were represented in the collection sent by M. Mouhot to his agent, Mr. S. Stevens, of Bloomsbury Street, London, and were the subject of several papers by Dr. Gray, Dr. Gunter, Dr. Louis Pfeiffer, and other naturalists, members of the Zoological Society of London, and published in the 'Annals and Magazine of Natural History.' At a meeting of the Royal Geographical Society on the 10th of March, 1862, Sir R. Murchison seized the occasion of reading some letters from the traveller relating to the topography of Cambodia, to pay a tribute of gratitude to his merit as a zoological collector and explorer. "His loss," he observed, "will be much felt by men of science, and a long time may elapse before another man will be found bold enough to follow his steps in that country of virgin forests and fever, and to the exploring of which he sacrificed his home, his health, and his life."

Mr. Stevens, in acquainting the brother of the traveller with the fact of his having received a new zoological collection which had been consigned to him, says, "I can truly say that the insects and shells equal, if they do not surpass, any in the most beautiful collections I have ever received, and show clearly what a marvellously rich country for the naturalist lies between Siam and Cochin-China." A splendid *scarabæus* was also sent to Mr. Stevens, who remarks, that " this insect was described in the 'Zoological Review' of Paris under the name of *Mouhotia gloriosa*, as a mark of respect to the late M. Mouhot, and stated to be one of the most magnificent known."

The Society of Montbéliard hastened, on the first news

of his death, to write to his brother, and the letter contains these words :—" His work was left unfinished, but it was gloriously commenced, and his name will not perish !"

Amidst all these eulogiums of a life, short but well spent, one of the most touching is a letter from M. Marie Ch. Fontaine, missionary at Saigon in Cochin-China, who was in Paris in August, 1862, and saw in a newspaper the death of the man whom he had met in Siam and Cambodia, which was soon confirmed by a letter from his brother. This worthy missionary addressed to M. Charles Mouhot a letter, of which the whole should be read; we only extract the following passage :—" I learned, when on my mission, the death of my father, and then that of my mother. I assure you that these two cruel blows scarcely made more impression on me than the news of the death of a man whose equal I had not met with during the twenty years that I have inhabited that country; and to hear of his dying without any help, and having no one near him but his servants throughout his illness, in a country so barbarous, was more than sufficient to make tears flow at the memory of this good and benevolent friend. Be assured, my dear Sir, that my sentiments are shared by all here who knew M. Mouhot. The natives themselves must have felt regret at his loss, for all whom he came near praised him for his behaviour towards them, and his gentleness and generosity; qualities invaluable in the eyes of that people."

In a letter recently addressed by Sir R. Schomburgh to M. C. Mouhot, enclosing the portraits of the King and

Queen of Siam, that gentleman thus expresses himself :—
" I admired the zeal and knowledge of your late brother;
and his manners were so amiable and modest that one
would have thought that every one with whom he came
in contact would have exercised all their influence to assist
him in his plans. I often regretted that he was not an
English subject, that I might have been able to do more
for him. I shall look impatiently for the publication of
his book, and have given orders that the French edition
may be forwarded to me at once."

I can add nothing to these touching testimonies, which
paint faithfully the man as I knew him in Holland. The
affectionate heart of Henri Mouhot awakened in others
an affection which the tomb does not destroy, but which
grows stronger with time.

J. J. BELINFANTE.

The Hague, December 15, 1862.

CONTENTS OF VOL. I.

CHAPTER V.

CHAPTER VI.

CHAPTER VII.

CHAPTER VIII.

CHAPTER IX.

CHAPTER X.

CHAPTER XI.

CHAPTER XII.

ILLUSTRATIONS TO VOL. I.

THE RIVER MENAM.

Drawn by M. Sabatier, from a Sketch by M. Mouhot.

TRAVELS IN INDO-CHINA,

ETC.

CHAPTER I.

The Voyage — First Impressions of Siam; and of Bangkok, its Capital—Reception in the Palace—The Two Kings of Siam.

On the 27th April, 1858, I embarked at London, in a sailing ship of very modest pretensions, in order to put in execution my long-cherished project of exploring the kingdoms of Siam, Cambodia, and Laos, and visiting the tribes who occupy the banks of the great river Mekon.

I spare the reader the details of the voyage and of my life on board ship, and shall merely state that there were annoyances in plenty, both as regards the accommodation for the passengers and the conduct of the captain, whose sobriety was more than doubtful.

We arrived at Singapore on the 3rd September. The census, taken in May, 1859, of the population of this beautiful and flourishing settlement, gave the following results.—Total, 81,792, of whom only 450 were Europeans, and 1995 Eurasians, or of a mixed race, such as Indo-English, Indo-Portuguese, and Indo-Dutch. The Chinese numbered 50,043, the Klings 11,735, and Malays 10,880; the women belonging to these races being computed at no more than 3248, 963, and 3700 respectively. The remainder of the population was composed of Bengalese 1236, Burmese and Siamese 14, Bugese 916, Javanese 3408, and Arabs 117.

There are in the island 13 schools, 70 temples or pagodas, 13 hotels and taverns, 26 pawnbrokers, 87 spirit-merchants, 144 houses licensed for opium-smoking, and 11 houses for the sale of a peculiar spirit unknown in France, but which is extracted from rice, and known under the name of arrack. The fishing-boats number 750. Facilities for locomotion and traffic are provided by 589 public carriages, 1180 passenger-boats, and 600 carts for the transport of merchandise.

In addition to the population of Singapore itself, the islands in the immediate vicinity, and forming a part of the settlement, contain 1500 inhabitants, making the entire population of Singapore and its dependencies nearly 83,000. I made only a short stay there, my chief object being to gain information respecting the country I was about to visit. On the 12th of the same month, after a very monotonous voyage, we arrived at the mouth of the river Menam, on whose banks Bangkok is built. A vast sandbank here bars the entrance of large ships, and compels them to go eight or nine miles farther up the gulf, and discharge their cargoes at great additional

VIEW IN THE GULF OF SIAM.

Drawn by M. Sabatier, from a Sketch by M. Mouhot.

expense. Our vessel, however, only drawing eight feet of water, passed without much difficulty, and anchored at Paknam in front of the Governor's house, whither the captain and myself proceeded without loss of time, in order to obtain the necessary permission to continue our route.

This formality over, I hastened to visit the forts, which are of brick and battlemented, the markets, and some of the streets. Paknam is the Sebastopol or Cronstadt of the Kings of Siam; nevertheless, I fancied that a European squadron could easily master it, and that the commander, after breakfasting there, might dine the same day at Bangkok.

On a little island in the middle of the river rises a famous and rather remarkable pagoda, containing, I was told, the bodies of their last kings. The effect of this pyramidal structure reflected in the deep and limpid water, with its background of tropical verdure, was most striking. As for the town, all that I saw of it was disgustingly dirty.

The Menam deserves its beautiful name—Mother of Waters—for its depth permits the largest vessels to coast along its banks without danger: so closely, indeed, that the birds may be heard singing gaily in the overhanging branches, and the hum of numberless insects enlivens the deck by night and day. The whole effect is picturesque and beautiful. Here and there houses are dotted about on either bank, and numerous villages give variety to the distant landscape.

We met a great number of canoes managed with

incredible dexterity by men and women, and often even
by children, who are here early familiarised with the water·
I saw the Governor's children, almost infants, throw
themselves into the river, and swim and dive like water-
fowl. It was a curious and interesting sight, particularly
from the strong contrast between the little ones and the
adults. Here, as in the whole plain of Siam, which I
afterwards visited, I met most attractive children, tempting
one to stop and caress them; but as they grow older they
rapidly lose all beauty, the habit of chewing the betel-
nut producing an unsightly blackening of the teeth and
swelling of the lips.

It is impossible to state the exact population of Bangkok,
the census of all Eastern countries being extremely imperfect. It is estimated, however, at from three to four
hundred thousand inhabitants. Owing to its semi-aquatic
site, we had reached the centre of the city while I
believed myself still in the country; I was only unde-
ceived by the sight of various European buildings, and the
steamers which plough this majestic river, whose margins
are studded with floating houses and shops.

Bangkok is the Venice of the East, and whether bent
on business or pleasure you must go by water. In place
of the noise of carriages and horses, nothing is heard but
the dip of oars, the songs of sailors, or the cries of the
Cipayes (Siamese rowers). The river is the high street
and the boulevard, while the canals are the cross streets,
along which you glide, lying luxuriously at the bottom of
your canoe.

GENERAL VIEW OF BANGKOK.

Drawn by M. Bocourt, from a Sketch by M. Mouhot.

We cast anchor in front of the cathedral of the French Mission and of the modest palace of Monseigneur Pallegoix, the worthy archbishop, who, for nearly thirty years, without any assistance but that of missionaries as devoted as himself, has made the revered emblem of Christianity and the name of France respected in these distant regions.

The sight of the Cross in foreign lands speaks to the heart like meeting with an old friend; one feels comforted and no longer alone. It is beautiful to see the devotion, self-denial, and courage of these poor and pious missionaries; a blessing as they are, also, to travellers, it would be ungrateful not to render them the gratitude which is their just due.

For some time past, particularly since the wars in China and Cochin-China, Siam has been much talked of in Europe; and, relying on the faith of treaties of peace and commerce, several French and English houses of business have been established there. Unfortunately, there was much deception on the part of the native authorities, which has given rise to general and well-founded complaints from the merchants. The fact is, that they have dangerous competitors in the mandarins and even in the princes, who monopolise the greater part of the trade in rice and sugar, their chief articles of commerce, which they despatch in their junks and other vessels. Moreover, the people were not prepared for the change which had taken place in the laws, and had scarcely cultivated more than enough for home consumption; add to this that the population is far from numerous, and, the Siamese being an indolent race, most of the agriculture falls into the hands of the Chinese, who flock to Singapore, Australia, and California.

The country certainly merits the reputation which it enjoys for beauty, but it is especially in its mountain scenery that nature displays its grandeur.

During a ten years' residence in Russia I witnessed the frightful effects of despotism and slavery. At Siam, results not less sad and deplorable obtruded themselves on my notice ; every inferior crouches before a higher in rank; he receives his orders kneeling, or with some other sign of abject submission and respect. The whole of society is in a state of prostration.

I was making my preparations for departure on the 16th October, my purpose being to penetrate into the north of the country and visit Cambodia and the savage tribes belonging to it, when I received an invitation from the King of Siam to be present at the great dinner which this monarch gives every year, on his birthday, to the European residents in Bangkok. I was presented by Monseigneur Pallegoix, and his Majesty's reception was kind and courteous. His costume consisted of a pair of large trousers, a short brown jacket of some thin material, and slippers; on his head he wore a little copper helmet like those worn by the naval officers, and at his side a rich sabre.

Most of the Europeans in Bangkok were present at the dinner, and enthusiastic toasts were drunk to the health

Drawn by M. Bocourt, from a Photograph

THE SECOND KING OF SIAM.

of his Majesty, who, instead of being seated, stood or walked round the table, chewing betel and addressing some pleasant observation to each of his guests in turn. The repast was served in a vast hall, from whence we could see a platoon of the royal guard, with flags and drums, drawn up in the courtyard. When I went to take leave of the King, he graciously presented me with a little bag of green silk, containing some of the gold and silver coin of the country,—a courtesy which was most unexpected, and for which I expressed my gratitude.

This King, whose official title is Somdel Phra, Paramanda, Maha-Mangkut—that is, His Majesty the King, encircled with the Great Crown—was born on the 18th October, 1804, and mounted the throne of Siam in the year 1851. The first part of his life was passed in complete retirement in a monastery, in this following the example of many of his predecessors: for all sects emanating from Buddhism think it necessary that the rulers of nations should prepare themselves for supreme power by a previous life of repose and sanctity.

It was only after the accession of Somdel Phra that the mastery he had gained over the most difficult sciences became known. After having applied himself to the history and geography of his country, he turned to the study of astronomy, natural philosophy, politics, and philology. He was familiar not only with all the dialects of Siam and Indo-China, but also with ancient Sanscrit and English, in which latter language he had written several treatises. The English journals at Hong-Kong have been honoured by articles from his pen, and no one who reads them can be surprised that the august contributor should have been elected a member of the Asiatic Society in London, a body which reckons on its list so many savans of the first rank.

His Majesty had also acquired a fair knowledge of Latin from the French missionaries, especially from Archbishop Pallegoix, who has been his friend for thirty years. He studied astronomy almost without a master, and had gained such proficiency in that science as to be able to calculate an eclipse and determine the latitude and longitude of a place. He introduced a printing-press into his dominions, in which both Siamese and Roman characters are used. His language testifies to his education and intelligence, though it more resembles the phraseology of books than that of ordinary conversation.

His predecessor had several hundred wives, and I believe the present King does not possess fewer than some dozen; but he only bestowed the title of queen on one, whose portrait hangs by the side of his own, and whose death, soon after my visit, left him inconsolable.

A singular institution, peculiar to Siam, Cambodia, and Laos, exists in a second king, slightly inferior to the other, and having a sort of reflected authority, the limits of which are not easily defined. His official title is Wangna, a word which literally signifies "the youngest King." He has his court, his mandarins, and his little army, and they pay him royal honours; but in reality he

TWO OF THE WIVES OF THE KING OF SIAM.

Drawn by M. H. Rousseau, from a Photograph.

is merely the first subject of his colleague. His sole prerogative is exemption from the customary prostration before the King, instead of which he salutes him by raising both hands in the air. It is true, he is allowed to draw largely from the royal treasury, but never without an order from the King, which, however, is rarely refused.

The present Wangna, Pin-Klau Chan You Hona, is the legitimate brother of the First King and his intended successor. He is a perfect gentleman, of a cultivated mind, writing and speaking English, and leading in his palace—which is arranged and furnished in our Western fashion—the life of a rich, noble, and learned European. He is fond of books and scientific researches, and familiar with all the improvements of modern civilization; he possesses in a higher degree than his brother the capacity for government and statesmanship, and deplores more than any one the sad condition in which his country languishes.

Before asking the reader to accompany me into the interior of Siam, it will not be amiss, in the next chapter, to give a short sketch of the kingdom itself and of its past history.

CHAPTER II.

THE name of Siam was first heard in Europe in the year 1502. Nine years after Alphonso d'Albuquerque had conquered the peninsula of Malacca, some intercourse took place between Portugal and Siam, which, however, was interrupted by the long wars between this country and the Burmese.

In 1632 an English vessel touched at the ancient capital Ayuthia. Shortly afterwards the Portuguese at Goa sent a party of Dominican and Franciscan missionaries to Siam, and the communication between the two nations became more frequent. The King engaged in his service three hundred Portuguese soldiers, who were distributed over the country, having lands allotted to them for cultivation, and who contracted marriage with native women. The missionaries built two churches, and established a school.

After a while the Dutch power began to supplant that of Portugal in the East, and, in the course of the seventeenth century, the empire of Siam was brought into contact with the new conquerors of the Indies. The Portuguese colonies gradually became extinct; and the influence of the Batavian settlers increased so much, that they esta-

blished at Ayuthia a Dutch factory, which, under its
director Schonten, attained its greatest prosperity about
the year 1690.   Various articles of merchandise were introduced into Siam, from whence, in return, were exported
skins, sapan-wood, &c. ; and the country, from its position
and the richness of its natural productions, became at
that time an important station for the commerce of the
Dutch between China and Japan, and the valuable islands
of Ceylon and Java.

France herself, at the height of her maritime power
under Louis XIV., could not equal the power of the
Dutch Company, though, at one period, chances eminently
favourable presented themselves to her.   A Greek adven-
turer named Constantine Phaulcon, of whom we shall have
subsequently to speak, opened for himself a remarkable
career in Siam, where he was converted to Romanism
by the missionaries.   He suggested to the King to send
envoys to Louis XIV., and their arrival in France produced a sensation, the echo of which we have heard in
our own day in the embassy from the same country to
Napoleon III.   His Most Christian Majesty replied by
accrediting ambassadors to the Siamese Court—De Chau-
mont in 1685, and La Loubéze in 1687.   Each was
accompanied by several Jesuit priests; and a force of 500
men, under the command of General de Fargues, was
stationed at Bangkok.   The General, however, was not
able to maintain his position ; Constantine met with a
tragic end, and the Jesuit fathers were kept as hostages.
These failures destroyed the French influence for more

than a century and a half, and for a time strengthened the power of Holland.

This brief glance at the intercourse between Europe and Siam in the sixteenth and seventeenth centuries will suffice.

The celebrated German traveller Mandelslohe visited the capital Ayuthia in 1537, and called it the Venice of the East—a title which, as we have seen, is equally applicable to the modern capital Bangkok. The Portuguese explorer Mendez Pinto, who also paid a visit to Siam in the sixteenth century, gives a favourable picture of the country, and all that has since come to our knowledge respecting it shows that he merited a greater faith in his statements than was accorded to him by his contemporaries.

The empire of Siam is of great extent. Its limits have varied much at different epochs of its history; and even now, with the exception of the western frontier, the lines of demarcation cannot be exactly traced, most of the border-lands being occupied by tribes more or less independent, and there are perpetual wars between the Malay and Burmese races on the one side, and the Cambodian or Chinese on the other. As nearly as can be calculated, the country extends, at present, from the 4th to the 20th or 22nd degree of north latitude, and from the 96th to the 102nd degree of east longitude ; and according to this computation, its length would be about 1200 miles and its breadth 400 miles.

The Siamese dominions are divided into forty-one pro-

PAGODA AT AYUTHIA.

Drawn by M. Thérond, from a Photograph.

vinces, each presided over by a phaja or governor, and these, again, are subdivided into numerous districts under the authority of functionaries of inferior rank, of whose administration little can be said in praise.

The northern provinces are five in number—Sangkalôk, Phitsalôk or Phitsanulôk, Kumphang-Phet, Phixai, and Tahëng. In the centre are nine provinces—Nantaburi or Jalat-Khuan, Pak-Pret, Patummatoni or Samkuk, Ayuthia or Krung-Kao, Ang-Thong, Monang-Phrom, Monang-In, Xainat, and Nakhon-Savan.

There are seven in the west—Monang-Pin, Suphan or Suphanaburi, Kan-Chanaburi or Pak-Phrëk, Rapri or Raxaburi, Nakhon-Xaisi, Sakhonburi or Tha-Chin, Samut-Songkhram or Mei-Khlong.

The eastern provinces number ten—Phetsjaboun, Bua-Xum, Sara-Buri, Nopha-Buri, Nakhon-Najok, Patsjin, Kabin, Sasong-Sao or Petriu, Battabâng, and Phanatsani-Khom.

In the south are—Pakhlat or Nakhon-Khuen-Khan, Paknam or Sananthaprakan, Bangplasor or Xalaburi, Rajong, Chantaboun or Chantabouri, Thung-Jai, Phiphri or Phetxaburi, Xumphon, Xaya, and Xalang or Salang.

Siam has been distinguished by the historians of the country under two great divisions—Monang-Nona, the region of the north, at first the more populous portion, and Monang-Tai, the southern region. The Chronicles of the south are sometimes called ' The Chronicles of the Royal City' (Ayuthia), and commence at the period when this place became the capital. De Barrios relates that, in his time (the fifteenth century), nine states were in subjection to the monarchs of Siam, two only of which were peopled by the Siamese race—viz., the southern kingdom, and that of the north, whose chief city was Chaumua. The Siamese language, likewise, was spoken only in these two countries.

Siam is called by the natives Thaï, or Monang-Thaï, which means "free" or "the kingdom of the free." Archbishop Pallegoix, who is a great authority in these matters, maintains that the modern name Siam is derived from Sajam, or "the brown race." *

While several districts in the north and east are tributary to this country, it appears to have been itself originally a great fief of China. Thus the King of Siam receives from this neighbouring empire a special confirmation of his authority, much resembling the patronage accorded by the Sultan to the Barbary states. However, if the external forms of this vassalage are observed, it is rather from a profound respect for tradition and ancient custom than from any virtual recognition of the power of the Emperor of China to acknowledge or interfere with the rights of sovereignty. One of the dependencies of this country, Cambodia, is also claimed by Cochin-China, and its ruler, unable to resist either of his more powerful neighbours, is forced to pay tribute to both.

---

* The word Siam is Malay, from which language this name, as well as many others of Indian places, has been borrowed by Europeans. The Siamese know it not.

SIAMESE WOMEN.

Drawn by M. Bocourt from a Photograph

The material originally positioned here is too large for reproduction in this reissue. A PDF can be downloaded from the web address given on page iv of this book, by clicking on 'Resources Available'.

The population of Siam cannot yet be determined with any great exactness, but it is certain that it bears no proportion to the extent of territory. Archbishop Pallegoix estimates it at only 6,000,000—a computation, however, very different from that of Sir John Bowring. The difficulty of arriving at any correct result is augmented by the Siamese custom of numbering only the men. Thus, the native registers showed, a few years ago, for the male sex, 2,000,000 Siamese, 1,000,000 Laotians, 1,000,000 Malays, 1,500,000 Chinese, 350,000 Cambodians, 50,000 Peguans, and a like number composed of various tribes inhabiting the mountain ranges.

In the north, a chain of mountains, covered with snow, extends from the province of Yunan to China, and its ramifications form two great divisions, between which is situated the fertile valley of Siam. Another chain stretches towards the west, as far as the Malay peninsula. The great river Menam, already mentioned, traverses the level country from north to south, taking its rise in the southern slopes of the mountains of Yunan, and empties itself into the Gulf of Siam. It is the Nile of this region, the great fertility of which is owing to the annual overflowing of its waters, an event eagerly looked for by the inhabitants, and welcomed as a blessing from Heaven. The Menam begins to rise in the month of June, and in August the inundation reaches its height, and then the waves of the ocean, opposing themselves to the current, force the waters of the river back upon its banks. The lands situated towards the middle of the great plain receive most benefit from this operation of nature, the higher districts being too much surrounded by mountains, while the lower are impregnated with so much salt water as to render the cultivation of rice difficult. If the regular inundations are, as a general rule, productive of immense benefit, they now and then, as in Egypt, lay waste the country : thus, for example, that of 1851 destroyed all the sugar-plantations ; and the water, to a depth of three or four feet, resting on the earth for some time, a large number of cattle perished, the rice-crops suffered seriously, and many valuable fruit-trees were carried away. Some years afterwards, however, in accordance with nature's beneficent law of compensation, the produce was only the more abundant.

The ancient annals of Siam relate that, about the seventh century, Chinese junks used to ascend the stream as far as Sang-Khalak, a distance of 120 leagues from the sea ; at present it is only navigable for 30 leagues at most. This alteration has arisen from a gradually-increasing collection of sand and alluvial deposit—a process which goes on in some of our western rivers, as, for instance, the Rhine and the Meuse.

The low grounds, as is usually the case in hot climates, are less healthy than the mountainous districts, and the forests especially are the seat of malignant fevers. Several other rivers, and numberless canals, fringed with bamboos and fruit-trees, round which fly a multitude of birds, give a pleasing aspect to the country, which is bounded on the horizon by richly-wooded hills.

Drawn by M. Sabatier, from a Sketch by M. Mouhot.

PERFORATED ROCK IN THE ISLE OF EBOULON, GULF OF SIAM.

The rivers are rich in fish, which, in addition to rice, forms the principal food of the people.

The shores of the sea are very picturesque, and the coast is studded with islands covered with the most luxuriant vegetation. " The Gulf of Siam," says Mgr. Pallegoix,

" is not subject to storms, nor to the destructive typhoons experienced on the Chinese seaboard; thus shipwrecks are of rare occurrence."

Sir John Bowring recommends to his countrymen a project which he believes feasible, and which would scarcely be secondary in importance to the intersection of the Isthmus of Darien or that of Suez. It is the union of the Bay of Bengal with the Gulf of Siam. He hopes that the establishment of amicable relations between Great Britain and the Siamese Empire will lead to the ventilation and eventual solution of a question so interesting both in a geographical and commercial point of view. It would be, in reality, as he says, a noble enterprise, which would considerably shorten the voyage between India and Eastern Asia, by making no longer necessary tne tedious détour through the Straits of Malacca, a passage which occupies not days, but weeks.

The soil of this country, composed in great part of alluvial earth, in Siam watered by its great river, and in Cambodia by the Nekong and many other streams, refreshed by the periodical rains, and glowing beneath a tropical sky, possesses almost unlimited capabilities. The mountains in the north contain precious metals, but the working of them is as yet very imperfectly attempted. The tin of Siam has been long in repute; copper, lead, and iron have also been discovered. Diamonds and other precious stones exist, although the exact localities where they are met with are not known, for the natives are very mysterious on the subject; but it is supposed that diamonds are found on the eastern boundary of the Gulf.

The history of the empire, arranged in the form of chronicles, is preserved in the archives, and not permitted to be inspected by strangers. The late king made investigations into these documents, which, previously to the foundation of Ayuthia, towards the middle of the fourteenth century, only presented a mass of confused materials, in which truth and fable are curiously intermingled, as in the annals of all nations, and pre-eminently those of the Orientals, who love to substitute highly-coloured narratives, in the style of the Arabian Nights, for plain history.

The Siamese trace their genealogy up to the first disciples of Buddha (Gandama), and commence their records five centuries before the Christian era. A succession of dynasties, varying their seat of government, figure in the earlier volumes; and the miracles of Buddha, and the intervention of supernatural beings, are frequently introduced. Later on there are accounts of matrimonial alliances between Siamese princes and the Imperial families of China, and of embassies to, and wars with, neighbouring countries, the whole interwoven with relations of prodigies and marvellous legends respecting Sudra and other divinities. After the establishment of Ayuthia as the capital, history assumes its rightful place, and the succession of the sovereigns and the course of events are registered with tolerable correctness. The city of Ayuthia was founded by Phaja-Utong, who took the title of Phra-Rama-Thibaldi.*

The following dates, drawn from the annals, and marking important epochs in the sacred history of Siam, are believed to be nearly correct:—

	Christian Era.		Buddhist Era.
The reigning Buddha died on the 3rd day of the 6th month of the year of the serpent, corresponding with the year B.C.	543		
The first great Buddhist Council was convoked under Ajatra-Sutra (in India) the year of the death of Buddha ..			
The second grand Council was convoked under Hala-Sokkaraja .. .. .. B.C.	443	.. ..	100
The third, under the rule of Sri Dhamma Soka .. .. B.C.	325	.. ..	218
The fourth grand Council .. .. B.C.	143	.. ..	400
The Buddhist doctor, Phra Buddha Ghosa, introduced Buddhism into Cambodia .. .. A.D.	422	.. ..	965

It was in the year 1000 of the Buddhist era, A.D. 457,

---

* " The word Phra, which so frequently occurs in this work, here appears for the first time; I have to remark that it is probably derived from, or of common origin with, the Pharaoh of antiquity. It is given in the Siamese dictionaries as synonymous with God, ruler, priest, and teacher. It is in fact the word by which sovereignty and sanctity are associated in the popular mind. As the title Divus was appropriated by the Roman Emperor, as in most monarchies a sort of sacredness is attached to the royal person, the orientals have made gods of their kings, their heroes, and their sages, without any scruple. Image-worship is in fact only the materialising or incarnating of the idea of Deity."—*The Kingdom and People of Siam*, Sir John Bowring.

Drawn by M. Catenacci, from a Photograph.

RUINS OF A TEMPLE AND STATUE OF BUDDHA AT AYUTHIA.

F 2

that King Tuang, whose accession and glorious reign had been announced by a communication from Gandama himself, and who possessed, in addition to his other claims to distinction, "a white elephant with black tusks," introduced the alphabet Tai, which was communicated to a numerous conclave of Buddhist priests. The ancient chronicles terminate with the establishment of Chao-Utonng in the new city of Si-Ayo-Thaya (Ayuthia), but leave the date of this event rather doubtful.

The following is the list of Siamese monarchs since the foundation of this capital :—

Siamese Era.		Christian Era.	
712	.. ..	1350	Phra Rama Phiobodi.
731	.. ..	1369	—— Rama Suen (his son).
732	.. ..	1370	—— Borom Raxa (his brother).
744	.. ..	1382	—— Rama Suen II.
747	.. ..	1385	—— Phaja Ram (his son).
763	.. ..	1401	Inthaxara.
792	.. ..	1430	Borom Raxa Phirat.
805	.. ..	1442	Boronua Irai Lokharat.
834	.. ..	1472	Phra Rama Phibodi.
875	.. ..	1513	Raxa Kuman.
876	.. ..	1514	Xaja Raxa Phirat.
889	.. ..	1527	Phra Jot Fa.
891	.. ..	1529	Maha Cha Kraphat Raxa Ihirat.
909	.. ..	1547	Phra Chao Xang Phuok.
914	.. ..	1552	Mahinthara Thirat.
926	.. ..	1564	Phra Naret.
957	.. ..	1595	Eka Thotsarot.
963	.. ..	1601	Chao Fa.
964	.. ..	1602	Phra Chao Song Iham.
989	.. ..	1627	Phra Chao Prasal Ihong.
1017	.. ..	1655	Chao Fa Xai.
1018	.. ..	1656	Phra Chao Xam Phuok.
1050	.. ..	1688	Phra Phet Raxa.

Siamese Era.		Christian Era.	
1059	.. ..	1697	Chao Dua.
1068	.. ..	1706	Name unknown.
1120	.. ..	1758	Chao Dok Ma Dua.
1128	.. ..	1766	Interregnum.
1129	.. ..	1767	Phyja Tak.
1173	.. ..	1811	Phra Phuti Chao Luang (the founder of the present dynasty).
1187	.. ..	1825	Phen Din Prasat Ihong.
1213	.. ..	1851	Phra Chao Prasat Ihong.

Instead of dwelling on the ancient history of Siam, we prefer to give an extract from the appendix to the celebrated work of Sir John Bowring, 'The Kingdom and People of Siam:' the passage originally appeared in 'The Chinese Repository,' and is from the pen of the late king:—

" Our ancient capital Ayuthia, before the year A.D. 1350, was but the ruin of an ancient place belonging to Kambuja (now known as Cambodia), formerly called Lawék, whose inhabitants then possessed Southern Siam, or Western Kambuja. Ayuthia is situated in lat. 14° 19' N., and long. 100° 37' E. from Greenwich. There were other cities, not far remote, also possessed by the Kambujans; but their precise locality or much of their history cannot now be satisfactorily ascertained. Some time near the year A.D. 1300, the former inhabitants were much diminished by frequent wars with the northern Siamese and the Peguans, or *Mous*, so that these cities were vacated, or left in a ruinous state, and nothing remained but their names.

" Former inhabitants declared that the people of

THE PAGODA OF AYUTHIA, FROM THE RIVER.

Drawn by M. Thérond, from a Photograph.

Chiang-rái, a province of what is now called Chiang-mái (North Laos), and Kampengpet, being frequently subjected to great annoyance from their enemies, deserted their native country, and formed a new establishment at Ch'á-liang, in the western part of Siam proper, and built a city, which they called Thepha-mahá-na-khon, whence has been preserved in the national records the name of our capital down to the present day, Krung-Thepha-mahá-na-khon. Their city was about lat. 16° N., and long. 99° E., and there five kings of the first dynasty reigned, until the sixth, named U-T'ong Rámá-thi-bodi, ascended the throne in 1344. This king, it is said, was son-in-law of his predecessor, who was named Sirichai Chiang Seu, who was without male issue, and therefore the throne descended to the son-in-law by right of the royal daughter.

" U-T'ong Rámá-thi-bodi was a mightier prince than any of his predecessors, and subsequently conquered and subjected to his sway all Southern Siam, and some provinces in the Malayan peninsula. He made Ch'á-liang the seat of his government for six years, and then, in consequence of the prevalence of disease of a pestilential character, he caused various researches to be made for some more healthy location, and finally fixed upon the site of Ayuthia, and there founded his new capital in April, 1350. This date is an ascertained fact. From this period our Siamese annals are more exact and the accounts generally reliable, being accompanied by dates of days, months, and years, from 1350 to 1767.

" Ayuthia, when founded, was gradually improved

and became more and more populous by natural increase, and the settlement there of families of Laos, Kambujans, Peguans, people from Yunnán in China, who had been brought there as captives, and by Chinese and Mussulmans from India, who came for the purposes of trade. Here reigned fifteen kings of one dynasty, successors of and belonging to the family of U-T'ong Rámá-thi-bodi, who, after his death, was honourably designated as Phra Chetha Bida—*i. e.* 'Royal Elder Brother Father.' This line was interrupted by one interloping usurper between the thirteenth and fourteenth. The last king was Mahíntrá-thi-rát. During his reign the renowned King of Pegu, named Chamna-dischop, gathered an immense army, consisting of Peguans, Burmese, and inhabitants of Northern Siam, and made an attack upon Ayuthia. The ruler of Northern Siam was Mahá-thamma rájá, related to the fourteenth king as son-in-law, and to the last as brother-in-law.

"After a siege of three months the Peguans took Ayuthia, but did not destroy it or its inhabitants, the Peguan monarch contenting himself with capturing the king and royal family, to take with him as trophies to Pegu, and delivered the country over to be governed by Mahá-thamma rájá, as a dependency. The King of Pegu also took back with him the oldest son of Mahá-thamma rájá as a hostage: his name was Phra Náret. This conquest of Ayuthia by the King of Pegu took place A.D. 1556.

" This state of dependence and tribute continued but

VIEW TAKEN FROM THE CANAL OF AYUTHIA.   Drawn by M. Thérond, from a Photograph.

a few years. The King of Pegu died, and in the confusion incident to the elevation of his son as his successor,
Prince Náret escaped with his family, and, attended by
many Peguans of influence, commenced his return to his
native land. The new king, on hearing of his escape,
despatched an army to seize and bring him back. They
followed him till he had crossed the Si-thong (Burman,
Sit-thaung) River, where he turned against the Peguan
army, shot the commander, who fell from his elephant
dead, and then proceeded in safety to Ayuthia.

" War with Pegu followed, and Siam again became
independent. On the demise of Mahá-thamma rájá, Prince
Náret succeeded to the throne, and became one of the
mightiest and most renowned rulers Siam ever had. In
his wars with Pegu he was accompanied by his younger
brother, Eká-tassa-rot, who succeeded Náret on the throne,
but, on account of mental derangement, was soon removed,
and Phra Siri Sin Wi-mon-tham was called by the nobles
from the priesthood to the throne. He had been very
popular as a learned and religious teacher, and commanded the respect of all the public counsellors ; but he
was not of the royal family. His coronation took place
A.D. 1602. There had preceded him a race of nineteen
kings, excepting one usurper. The new king submitted
all authority in government to a descendant of the former
line of kings, and to him also he intrusted his sons for
education, reposing confidence in him as capable of
maintaining the royal authority over all the tributary
provinces. This officer thus became possessed of the

highest dignity and power. His master had been raised
to the throne at an advanced age. During the twenty-six
years he was on the throne he had three sons, born under
the royal canopy —*i. e.* the great white umbrella, one of
the insignia of royalty.

"After the demise of the king, at an extreme old age,
the personage whom he had appointed as regent, in full
council of the nobles, raised his eldest son, then sixteen
years old, to the throne. A short time after the regent
caused the second son to be slain, under the pretext of
a rebellion against his elder brother. Those who were
envious of the regent, excited the king to revenge his
brother's death as causeless, and plan the regent's assas-
sination; but he, being seasonably apprised of it, called a
council of the nobles and dethroned him after one year's
reign, and then raised his youngest brother, the third
son, to the throne.

"He was only eleven years old. His extreme youth
and fondness for play, rather than politics or government, soon created discontent. Men of office saw that it
was exposing their country to contempt, and sought for
some one who might fill the place with dignity. The
regent was long accustomed to all the duties of the
government, and had enjoyed the confidence of their late
venerable king; so, with one voice, the child was dethroned
and the regent exalted under the title of Phra Chau Pra
Sath-thong. This event occurred A.D. 1630.

"The king was said to have been connected with the
former dynasty, both paternally and maternally; but the

RUINS OF A PAGODA AT AYUTHIA.

Drawn by M. Therond, from a Photograph.

connection must have been quite remote and obscure. Under the reign of the priest-king he bore the title Raja Suriwong, as indicating a remote connection with the royal family. From him descended a line of ten kings, who reigned at Ayuthia and Lopha-buri—Louvo of French writers. This line was once interrupted by an usurper between the fourth and fifth reigns. This usurper was the foster-father of an unacknowledged though real son of the fourth king Chau Nárái. During his reign many European merchants established themselves and their trade in the country, among whom was Constantine Phaulkon (Faulkon). He became a great favourite through his skill in business, his suggestions and superintendence of public works after European models, and by his presents of many articles regarded by the people of those days as great curiosities, such as telescopes, &c.

"King Nárái, the most distinguished of all Siamese rulers, before or since, being highly pleased with the services of Constantine, conferred on him the title of Chau Phyá Wicha-yentrá-thé-bodi, under which title there devolved on him the management of the government in all the northern provinces of the country. He suggested to the king the plan of erecting a fort on European principles as a protection to the capital. This was so acceptable a proposal, that at the king's direction he was authorised to select the location and construct the fort.

" He selected a territory which was then employed as garden-ground, but is now the territory of Bangkok. On the west bank, near the mouth of a canal, now called

Báng-luang, he constructed a fort, which bears the name of Wichayeiw Fort to this day. It is close to the residence of his Royal Highness Chaufá-noi Kromma Khun Isaret rangsan. This fort and circumjacent territory was called Thana-buri. A wall was erected, enclosing a space of about 100 yards square. Another fort was built on the east side of the river, where the walled city of Bangkok now stands. The ancient name Bángkôk was in use when the whole region was a garden.* The above-mentioned fort was erected about the year A.D. 1675.

"‚This extraordinary European also induced his grateful sovereign King Nárái to repair the old city of Lophaburi (Louvo), and construct there an extensive royal palace on the principles of European architecture. On the north of this palace Constantine erected an extensive and beautiful collection of buildings for his own residence. Here also he built a Romish church, on which are still to be seen some inscriptions in European letters, supposed to be Dutch or German; they assuredly are neither French nor English (perhaps they are Greek, as he was of Greek extraction, and born at Cephalonia). The ruins of all these edifices and their walls are still to be seen, and are said to be a great curiosity. It is moreover stated that he planned the construction of canals, with reservoirs at intervals for bringing water from the mountains on the north-east to the city Lopha-

---

* Such names abound now, as Bang-cha, Bang-phra, Bang-plá-soi, &c.; *Báng* signifying a small stream or canal, such as is seen in gardens.

THE GREAT TOWER OF THE PAGODA WAT-CHING AT BANGKOK.

The material originally positioned here is too large for reproduction in this reissue. A PDF can be downloaded from the web address given on page iv of this book, by clicking on 'Resources Available'.

buri, and conveying it through earthen and copper pipes and syphons, so as to supply the city in the dry season on the same principle as that adopted in Europe. He commenced also a canal, with embankments, to the holy place called Phra-Bat, about twenty-five miles south-west from the city. He made an artificial pond on the summit of Phra-Bat mountain, and thence, by means of copper tubes and stop-cocks, conveyed abundance of water to the kitchen and bath-rooms of the royal residence at the foot of the mountain. His works were not completed when misfortune overtook him.

" Many Siamese officers and royal ministers were jealous of his influence, and murmured their suspicions of his being a secret rebel. At length he was accused of designing to put the king to death by inviting him to visit the church he had built, between the walls of which, it is said, he had inserted a quantity of gunpowder, which was to be ignited by a match at a given signal, and thus involve the death of the king. On this serious charge he was assassinated by private order of the king. (This is the traditional story: the written annals state that he was slain in his sedan while faithful to his king, by order of a rebel prince, who perceived he could not succeed in his nefarious plans against the throne while Constantine lived.) The works which he left half done are now generally in ruins, viz. the canal to Phra-Bat and the aqueduct at the mountains.

" After the demise of Nárái, his unacknowledged son, born of a princess of Yunnan or Chiang-Mai, and intrusted for training to the care of Phya Petcha raja, slew Nárái's son and heir, and constituted his foster-father king, himself acting as prime minister till the death of his foster-father, fifteen years after; he then assumed the royal state himself. He is ordinarily spoken of as Nai Dua. Two of his sons and two of his grandsons subsequently reigned at Ayuthia. The youngest of these grandsons reigned only a short time, and then surrendered the royal authority to his brother and entered the priesthood. While this brother reigned, in the year 1759, the Burman king, Meng-luang Alaung Barah-gyi, came with an immense army, marching in three divisions on as many distinct routes, and combined at last in the siege of Ayuthia.

" The Siamese king, Chaufa Ekadwat Anurak Moutri, made no resolute effort of resistance. His great officers disagreed in their measures. The inhabitants of all the smaller towns were indeed called behind the walls of the city, and ordered to defend it to their utmost ability; but jealousy and dissension rendered all their bravery useless. Sallies and skirmishes were frequent, in which the Burmese were generally the victorious party. The siege was continued for two years. The Burmese commander-in-chief, Mahá Nōratha, died, but his principal officers elected another in his place. At the end of the two years the Burmese, favoured by the dry season, when the waters were shallow, crossed in safety, battered the walls, broke down the gates, and entered without resistance. The provisions of the Siamese were exhausted, confusion reigned, and the Burmese fired the city and

public buildings.   The king, badly wounded, escaped with
his flying subjects, but soon died alone of his wounds and
his sorrows.   He was subsequently discovered and buried.

" His brother, who was in the priesthood and now the
most important personage in the country, was captured
by the Burmans, to be conveyed in triumph to Burmah.
They perceived that the country was too remote from
their own to be governed by them; they therefore freely
plundered the inhabitants, beating, wounding, and even
killing many families, to induce them to disclose treasures
which they supposed were hidden by them.   By these
measures the Burmese officers enriched themselves with
most of the wealth of the country.   After two or three
months spent in plunder they appointed a person of Mon
or Peguan origin as ruler over Siam, and withdrew with
numerous captives, leaving this Peguan officer to gather
fugitives and property to convey to Burmah at some
subsequent opportunity.   This officer was named Phrá
Nái Kông, and made his head-quarters about three miles
north of the city, at a place called Phō Sam-ton, *i. e.* ' the
three Sacred Fig-trees.'   One account relates that the
last king mentioned above, when he fled from the city
wounded, was apprehended by a party of travellers and
brought into the presence of Phyá Nái Kông in a state
of great exhaustion and illness; that he was kindly
received and respectfully treated, as though he was still
the sovereign; and that Phyá Nái Kông promised to
confirm him again as ruler of Siam, but his strength
failed and he died a few days after his apprehension.

"The conquest by Burmah, the destruction of Ayuthia, and appointment of Phyá Nái Kông, took place in March, A.D. 1767. This date is unquestionable. The period between the foundation of Ayuthia and its overthrow by the Burmans embraces 417 years, during which there were thirty-three kings of three distinct dynasties, of which the first dynasty had nineteen kings with one usurper, the second had three kings, and the third had nine kings and one usurper.

"When Ayuthia was conquered by the Burmese, in March, 1767, there remained in the country many bands of robbers associated under brave men as their leaders. These parties had continued their depredations since the first appearance of the Burman army, and during about two years had lived by plundering the quiet inhabitants, having no government to fear. On the return of the Burman troops to their own country, these parties of robbers had various skirmishes with each other during the year 1767.

"The first king established at Bangkok was an extra-ordinary man, of Chinese origin, named Pin Tat. He was called by the Chinese Tia Sin Tat, or Tuat. He was born at a village called Bánták, in Northern Siam, in lat. 16° N. The date of his birth was in March, 1734. At the capture of Ayuthia he was thirty-three years old. Previous to that time he had obtained the office of second governor of his own township, Ták, and he next obtained the office of governor of his own town, under the dignified title of Phyá Ták, which name he bears to

PRIEST'S HOUSE NEAR AYUTHIA.

Drawn by M. Thérond, from a Photograph.

the present day. During the reign of the last King of
Ayuthia, he was promoted to the office and dignity
of governor of the city of Kam-Cheng-philet, which
from times of antiquity was called the capital of the
western province of Northern Siam. He obtained this
office by bribing the high minister of the king, Chaufá
Ekadwat Anurak Moutri; and being a brave warrior, he
was called to Ayuthia on the arrival of the Burman
troops, as a member of the council. But when sent to
resist the Burman troops, who were harassing the eastern
side of the city, perceiving that the Ayuthian government was unable to resist the enemy, he, with his
followers, fled to Chautaburi (Chautabun), a town on the
eastern shore of the Gulf of Siam, in lat. $12\frac{1}{2}°$ N. and
long. 101° 21' E. There he united with many brave
men, who were robbers and pirates, and subsisted by
robbing the villages and merchant-vessels. In this way
he became the great military leader of the district, and
had a force of more than ten thousand men. He soon
formed a treaty of peace with the headman of Báng-
plásoi, a district on the north, and with Kambuja and
Annam (or Cochin China) on the south-east."

Such is the short historical sketch, given by the late
King of Siam, up to this date, and which we must complete from other sources.

As much by stratagem as by force of arms, he gained
possession of the northern districts; but, not deeming
himself secure enough from hostile attacks in that part of
the country, he decided on falling back towards the south,

and established himself at Bangkok, having previously surprised and put to death Phrá-Nai-Kông, the Burman governor of that place, and seized on a quantity of money, provisions, and ammunition. Its proximity to the sea afforded many advantages, one being that escape would be tolerably easy should fortune prove adverse to him. He there built a palace on the western bank of the river, near the fort, which is now standing.

After various encounters with the Burmans, he reduced them into subjection, mainly through the assistance of his flotilla; and on one occasion he overpowered their whole camp, recovering great part of the booty they had amassed, and finally freeing the country from those bitter foes, who had brought into it so much desolation and terror. The people, in gratitude to their deliverer, gladly aided him in his assumption of royal authority. He issued his mandates from Bangkok, appointed viceroys, and distributed colonists far and wide for the repeopling of the country. Thus, by the end of 1768, he found himself sovereign of all the southern part of Siam and the eastern provinces on the shores of the Gulf.

Profiting by a sanguinary war between China and Burmah, he reconquered the northern district of Horahh. He had still to contend with a revolt organised by a prince of the old dynasty, who, pending the struggle with the Burmans, had taken refuge in Ceylon. This, however, was soon quelled; and two more provinces were recovered, which had taken advantage of the foreign invasion to assert their independence. At the end of three years

Vol. I, p. 90.　　　　　DETAILS OF THE PAGODA WAT-CHANG AT BANGKOK.

The material originally positioned here is too large for reproduction in this reissue. A PDF can be downloaded from the web address given on page iv of this book, by clicking on 'Resources Available'.

Phya-Jak was master of the whole of the north, and had everywhere re-established peace and order. His dominion being now set on a firm foundation, it was a comparatively easy matter successfully to resist a new attack of the Burmans in 1771; and the year following he sent an expedition into the Malay peninsula to take possession of Lagor, whose governor, formerly a vassal of the king, had assumed the sovereignty, and proclaimed Phya-Jak a usurper. The governor, being worsted in several engagements, took refuge with the chief of Patawi, a town in the peninsula, by whom he was surrendered to the followers of Phya-Jak. The king himself, meanwhile, had entered Lagor, made captives of all the governor's family, and carried off his treasures. Among his relatives was a daughter possessed of great beauty: the King gave her a place in his harem; and, through her intercession, her father and all the family were spared. Three or four years afterwards she procured his reinstatement as prince of that district, which at the present day is governed by his descendants.

Phya-Jak's reign did not end happily: in the latter part of his life he fell into a state of morbid melancholy, treated his subjects with cruelty, and lost his popularity. One of his generals, Chakri, commanding in Cambodia, took advantage of these circumstances to concert a plot against the King, who was taken prisoner at Bangkok, and assassinated in the year 1782. Chakri ascended the throne, and, dying soon afterwards, was succeeded by his son. The old quarrels with the Burmans were renewed about some disputed districts on the northern frontier; and the Siamese monarch came victoriously out of two encounters, but, in a third, was overcome, and lost the western part of the country lying towards Burmah.

This king died in 1809, and his son and successor, fearing, or feigning to dread, conspiracies against him, put to death one hundred and seventeen Siamese nobles, among whom were several generals who had fought by his father's side against the Burmans. This atrocious massacre, and the murder of a cousin much beloved by the people, alienated their affections from him. In other respects he ruled with wisdom and moderation: keeping in check the turbulent Malays, he also successfully repulsed the incursions of the Burmans, bringing his prisoners to Bangkok, where he gave them lands to cultivate, and thus extended his capital.

The English Government, wishing to form a commercial treaty with this prince, sent Mr. Crawfurd on a mission to Siam; but although that gentleman obtained much interesting information respecting the country, he failed in attaining his purpose. Allowed to remain with his suite for some time at Bangkok, they were treated rather as prisoners than guests. Their propositions were rejected; and the only concession obtained from his Majesty was a promise not to increase the export and import duties, the entire abolition of which had been the object of the negotiation. The King died in 1824, and was succeeded by his illegitimate son, Crom-Chiat.

This prince, although he feared the English, saw the

Drawn by M. Catenacci, from a Photograph.

RUINS AT AYUTHIA.

advantages of an extended commerce, and, in 1826, concluded a treaty with Great Britain, then represented by Captain Burney; but it did not effect all that had been desired. Direct mercantile intercourse between the two countries was certainly guaranteed, and assistance in all cases of shipwreck on the coast; but English subjects, during their stay, were to be subject to the laws of the empire; and in each province the commerce could be extended or limited at the will of the governor. As these functionaries constantly infringed the terms of the treaty, and imposed heavy charges on the native articles exported, as well as on British goods introduced, disappointment naturally resulted; and the Siamese, fearing a resort to arms on the part of England, made preparations for defence, and fortified the mouth of the Menam.

Meanwhile France was attempting to resume her old intercourse with Siam; but at first great distrust was manifested of the Catholic missionaries. In 1780 they had been ordered, on pain of death, to quit the kingdom; they retired for a time, but again gradually insinuated themselves, and met with considerable success. We owe to Mgr. Pallegoix, in addition to an interesting relation of the progress of the mission, very important information concerning this empire in the far East—its literature, and the character and the manners of the inhabitants. He established there seven churches and four chapels; a seminary in which are thirty native pupils, several other schools, and four monasteries; and has baptized eight thousand Siamese. The King, annoyed at the

advance of the new religion, issued, in 1848, an edict
against the missionaries, commanding the destruction of
all their places of worship; but it was very partially
carried into execution.

The Protestant mission has had a more restricted
sphere of action. The celebrated Dr. Gutzlaff made a
long stay at Bangkok in 1828, and finished there his
translation of the New Testament into Siamese. This
work was published at Singapore, and has since been
widely circulated. In 1830 he revisited Siam, and translated the greater part of the Scriptures into the languages of Cambodia and Laos. At his request the
American Baptists founded the first Protestant mission at
Siam; the Presbyterians established a second in 1840;
and a third was founded, in 1850, by the Society of the
American Board of Commissioners for Foreign Missions.
Their labours, however, have not yet been crowned with
any great success; nevertheless, by uniting to their
ministerial office the practice of medicine, they have
done much good, and been favourably received by the
people.

The French priests have recently made efforts to gain
an influence over the government of Siam. At the death
of the King Orom-Chiat, his son Chao-Fa, then twenty
years of age, should have been his rightful successor, but
an elder illegitimate son seized on the throne, promising
his brother to resign it in a few years. This promise not
having been fulfilled, the prince, as we have before mentioned, went into complete retirement, and gave himself

up to scientific pursuits. He then came into contact with the Catholic missionaries, and, at their persuasion, made himself acquainted with their religion.

In 1851 the King fell ill, and, in spite of the promise to his brother, wished to appoint one of his own sons as his successor; but he was answered that the country had already a sovereign; and, on his decease, Prince Chao-Fa mounted the throne, under the name of Somdet Phra. Mgr. Pallegoix addressed to him a letter of congratulation, and presented him with a portrait of Louis Napoleon, then President of the French Republic. The King, in return, made him a gift of money, and revoked the decree of banishment against the five Catholic priests; and at an audience granted to the bishop before his departure for Europe, in 1852, he charged him with messages to Prince Louis Napoleon and the Pope,— intrusting to him an autograph letter for the latter, written in English, and expressing a great regard for his Holiness, as well as his resolution to grant full toleration in his kingdom to the Catholic religion.

He also declared to the archbishop * his intention of assuring to his subjects entire religious liberty, with which view he made inquiries from time to time respecting the work of the Catholic missionaries, so as to protect the converted natives against the heathen governors. From that time the friendship with France has never

---

* Mgr. Pallegoix died April, 1862, at Bangkok, where the king had him buried with great pomp.

been interrupted, but has become more and more intimate.

Negotiations were commenced at Bangkok in 1856, in the name of the French Government, which terminated in a highly satisfactory manner, a treaty of friendship and commerce being signed on the 15th August between the two countries, which was ratified in the following year. The reception accorded to M. de Montigny, the French envoy, on this occasion by the two kings, was as brilliant as it was cordial; nor was he entertained less kindly by any of the authorities with whom he came in contact, which proved that Siam has preserved a pleasing remembrance of the embassies exchanged with Louis XIV.

All this augured favourably for the future friendly relations between the two Crowns; and these were confirmed in the year 1861, when his Siamese Majesty sent an embassy to Paris, where it arrived in June, and was received with great magnificence.

A French publication * gave the following account of the commerce with Siam:—"According to the information obtained from M. de Montigny, the commercial and maritime relations between the kingdom of Siam and Europe are capable of great development. Already more than sixty European ships have since 1854 entered yearly the port of Bangkok, to which must be added a considerable number of junks and *prahus*, which navigate

---

* 'L'Annuaire des Deux Mondes.' 1856-1857.

SIAMESE LADIES AT DINNER.

Drawn by M. Bocourt, from a Photograph

The material originally positioned here is too large for reproduction in this reissue. A PDF can be downloaded from the web address given on page iv of this book, by clicking on 'Resources Available'.

the China Sea and the Malayan Archipelago. The
markets of Siam and Laos abound in natural products,
such as tobacco, cotton, sugar, spice, and dyes. The
forests abound with magnificent trees, particularly teak.
By the terms of the treaty with France, the duties,
whether import or export, are but three per cent. on the
value of the merchandise. There is therefore room for
hope that commerce, favoured by the moderation of this
tariff, will rapidly increase, and that the French navy
will profit by it."

In 'Les Annales du Commerce Extérieur' we find the
following account:—" The greater part of the commerce
of Siam, Laos, and Cambodia is in the hands of the
Chinese, who are much more active and intelligent than
the natives. Their mercantile transactions are generally
characterised by dishonesty, and we cannot too strongly
warn our traders against the frauds of every kind common
in this country, such as mixing diverse qualities, adultera-
tion, and saturating various articles with moisture to
increase the weight. Raw silk, cotton, and hemp, tobacco,
and other merchandise sold by weight, should be carefully
examined when delivered, and always compared with the
samples, which it is prudent to demand beforehand. The
treaty concluded between the Siamese Government and
France abolishes all monopolies, and obliges the authorities to watch over the strict and faithful execution of
all bargains; therefore, in case of fraud, traders should
show a bold face and demand indemnity. They should
be careful themselves to set an example of strict probity,

this being the surest way to improve the morality of the Siamese merchants, who, in dealing with people of proved honesty, will have less temptation to employ fraud.

" The best commerce will be, doubtless, that of barter ; but it will be difficult to carry this to any great extent, as these people have few wants. Their ordinary dress, for example, consists simply of drawers in the hot season, to which in winter they add one or more scarves, to cover the upper part of the body. The dignitaries and wealthy individuals on state occasions wear a rich suit, consisting of drawers, vest, belt, and a large tunic. They go barefoot, rarely having even sandals. They are not of a migratory nature, but have their fixed habitations, and are fond of elegance and luxury. Very imitative in their ways, they feel a pride in putting on a European dress; and some of those made after the fashion of Louis XIV.'s reign are still preserved, especially among the descendants of the Portuguese, who are numerous. The uniforms of the soldiers are copied from those of Europe; and the whole nation has a great taste for our Parisian furniture, cotton, silk, and woollen fabrics, porcelain, china, glass, bronzes, cutlery, ironmongery, and toys. Other articles in much esteem with them, and exported by us, are fire-arms, side-arms, saddlery, quilts, carpets, clocks, and windows. Our champagne, brandy, gin, and kirsch, would find in Siam a certain and ready sale in exchange for the produce of the country."

The efforts of the Americans to obtain from the

SIAMESE ROPE-DANCER.

Siamese Government favourable terms of commerce were for a time fruitless, but in 1833 a treaty was concluded with the United States, which proved of but little material benefit. A second embassy from the Western Republic failed completely. Balestier, the envoy, could not even obtain an audience from the king, and consequently was unable to deliver his letters of credit. The Americans had been unfortunate in their choice of Balestier as their representative, he having formerly been in a mercantile house at Singapore, and in no favour either with the king or his ministers. A treaty was, however, eventually concluded between the two nations.

Sir James Brooke, the English ambassador at Bangkok, found his advances coldly received. Possibly the Court felt aggrieved by the attitude assumed by that gentleman ; but, whatever may have been the reason, matters nearly approached to an open rupture. In September, 1850, he abandoned the negotiation, and Great Britain and Siam remained estranged, until the English Government, desirous to establish friendly relations with the Eastern monarch, despatched Sir John Bowring to Bangkok, with instructions to arrange a commercial treaty, which he effected in 1855. His travels have been published in two volumes, and contain, perhaps, the most accurate and full information we possess of Siam. It was particularly from his acquaintance with the language and manners of the nation that Sir John Bowring acquitted himself so well of his task. He was received at Court with great favour, and had several interviews with the

king, whose thirst for knowledge pleased him, and whose
good will he managed to secure. In all his negotiations
with the Siamese ministers he displayed skill and adroit-
ness. Knowing by experience what would be the most
profitable conditions, he succeeded in effecting the rati-
fication of an advantageous agreement on the 18th April,
1855, by which the Crown of Siam consented to the appointment of a British consul at the capital, and granted
entire liberty of commerce to English merchants in all
the maritime districts of the empire. All duties were
lowered; those upon opium almost entirely abolished,
provision being made that this article should only be
sold to parties specially licensed by the Government.
On the other hand, the English traders might purchase
all the productions of the country directly from the pro-
ducer. It is only in times of scarcity that the king
reserves to himself the right of forbidding the exportation of rice, salt, and fish. English subjects are permitted
to settle at Bangkok, to hold landed property there,
build or purchase houses, and to lease land to others;
but this last privilege is only accorded after a ten years'
possession.

Full toleration in religious matters was guaranteed; and
if the presence of a British ship of war was at any time
thought requisite for protection of their interests, it was
permitted to lie in the Gulf, but not to pass beyond
Paknam without express leave from the Government.

Holland has also renewed her ancient dealings with
the country, and ratified a treaty during the present year

(1862).   Even before the arrival of the Siamese ambassadors in Europe, a French publication * said very justly,
" The Government of Siam is showing itself more and
more favourable towards Europeans, who find at Bangkok
not only protection, but sympathy and toleration for
their religion.   Bangkok has become one of the most considerable markets of Asia; and the kingdom of Siam is
reaping the reward of the liberal politics which it has
introduced into the extreme East, and which is warmly
seconded by France, England, and the United States."

---

* 'L'Annuaire des Deux Mondes.'   1858-1859.

CHAPTER III.

AFTER my visits of ceremony to the two kings, I hastened to finish the preparations for my voyage. I bought a light boat capable of holding all my chests, reserving a narrow space for myself, and another for the bipeds and quadrupeds forming my adopted family—viz., two rowers, one of whom also officiated as cook, a parroquet, an ape, and a dog. One of the boatmen was a Cambodian, and the other an Annamite, both Christians, and knowing a few words of Latin * and English, so that, as I had already picked up a little Siamese, I could make myself pretty well understood.

On the 19th October I quitted Bangkok, and commenced my voyage up the Menam. The current runs very strongly at this season, and it took us five days to go about seventy miles. At night we suffered terribly from the mosquitoes, and even during the day had to keep up an incessant fanning to drive off these pestilent little vampires. They were so numerous that you could catch

---

* Latin is much esteemed among the native Christians, thanks to the ritual of the Catholic mission.

THE INUNDATION OF THE MENAM.

Drawn by M. Sabatier, from a Sketch by M. Mouhot.

them by handfuls, and their humming resembled that of
a hive of bees. These insects are the curse of all tropical
countries, but here they peculiarly abound in the marshes
and lands covered with slime and mud left by the retiring
waters, where the heat of the sun and the moisture combined, favour their rapid increase. My legs suffered
especially from their attacks.

As the country was entirely inundated, we could not
land anywhere, and even after killing a bird I frequently
could not get at it. All this was very tantalising, for the
banks of the stream are very gay and attractive, nature
wearing here her richest dress.

At this time of the year the rains have entirely
ceased, and do not return for several months. For some
days the north-eastern monsoon had been blowing, the
weather was constantly fine, and the heat tempered by
the wind. The waters, also, were beginning to subside.
It was the period of the religious *fêtes* of the Siamese,
and the river was almost incessantly crowded with long
and handsome boats bearing flags, many of them manned
by more than fifty rowers, all in new and bright-coloured
dresses, trying to pass each other, and exciting themselves
by piercing cries and all sorts of noises. In some cases,
however, sweet and agreeable music formed an accompaniment more grateful to the ear. One boat, belonging
to a mandarin, was escorted by a number of others; it
was remarkable for its elaborate carving and the magnificence of its gilding, and was carrying yellow stuffs
and other presents to the neighbouring pagodas.

The king rarely shows himself in public more than twice a year, once during the month of October, and a second time on board his barge, when a procession is formed consisting of three or four hundred boats, often containing more than 1200 persons. The effect produced by this aquatic pageant, with the rowers in their brilliant dresses, and the multitude of rich flags, is extremely gorgeous, and such as is only to be witnessed in the East.

I was surprised to see the gaiety and light-heartedness of the people, in spite of the yoke which weighs on them and the exorbitant taxes they have to pay; but the softness of the climate, the native gentleness of the race, and the long duration of their servitude from generation to generation, have made them oblivious of the bitterness and hardships inseparable from despotism.

Everywhere they were making preparations for their fishing season, for when the waters subside from the fields, the fish are most plentiful. Dried in the sun, they furnish food for the whole year, and are also exported in large quantities. My boat was so encumbered with chests, boxes, and instruments, that the space left for me was very confined, and I suffered from heat and want of air; but these were trifles compared with the mosquitoes.

On arriving at Ayuthia, my rowers conducted me direct to the excellent Father Larmandy, a French missionary, by whom I was expected. The good priest received me with great kindness, and placed at my disposal all he had to offer in his little house. He employs his leisure time in the study of natural history and in hunting, and

RUINS OF A PAGODA AT AYUTHIA. Drawn by M. Beaumont, from a Photograph.

frequently accompanied me in my rambles. As we explored the woods we talked of our own charming country —France.

After a long hunting or rowing expedition, we always, on our return home, found our repast prepared by my servant Niou, who excelled in Siamese cookery, and which our fatigue made us doubly appreciate. Rice and omelette, or curried fish, bamboo-stalks, haricots, and other wild vegetables, formed our diet, with the addition of roast fowls and game when the chase had been fortunate. Three chickens cost a "fuand" (37 centimes).

The heat was sometimes overwhelming; for a week we had 90 degrees of Fahrenheit in the shade throughout the twenty-four hours, but the mosquitoes were fewer in number, which was a great relief. In our excursions we visited some ruins amid the woods, and I made a collection of beautiful butterflies, and found several insects new to me. When I reach Pakpriau, which is a few days' journey to the north, on the frontier of the lake, I shall find a mountain country, where I am sure of a plentiful harvest of insects and land shells.

The comet, which I had already observed on my journey, shone here with increased brilliancy, and it was difficult not to believe that the extreme heat was owing to the influence of this meteor.

I drank nothing but tea, hoping by abstinence from cold water and from all wine and spirits, to escape fever. So far, my health had certainly never been better, not even in the north of Russia. Since the ports have been opened to English and other European vessels everything has been doubled in price, but still remained cheap as compared with Europe, and I did not spend more than a franc a day for my own living and that of my men. The people flocked to see my collections, and could not imagine what I should do with so many animals and insects. I have before mentioned the skilful management of boats, and the fearlessness in swimming and diving, displayed by very young children. I used to amuse myself by offering some of them my cigar-ends to smoke, in return for which they would run after butterflies, and bring them to me uninjured.

I discovered here a sort of spider, which is also, I believe, found at the Cape, from which a silken thread may be drawn out by taking hold of the end hanging from its body. One has but to go on winding; the thread is very strong, and never breaks.

It requires some time to become accustomed to the shrill chirpings during the night of myriads of grasshoppers and other insects, which seem never to sleep. There appears to be no such thing as silence or repose; everywhere is a continual stir, the gushing overflow of life in this exuberant region.

What a contrast between the subdued tints and cold skies of Europe, and this burning clime and glittering firmament! How pleasant it was to rise in the early morning before the glowing sun had begun his course; and sweeter still in the evening to listen to the thousand

ELEPHANTS IN AN ENCLOSURE OR "PARK" AT AYUTHIA.

Drawn by M. T. Lamge from a Sketch by M. Mouhot.

Vol. I, p. 144.

The material originally positioned here is too large for reproduction in this reissue. A PDF can be downloaded from the web address given on page iv of this book, by clicking on 'Resources Available'.

sounds, the sharp and metallic cries, which seemed as though an army of goldsmiths were at work!

The people here might be extremely happy, were they not kept in such abject slavery; bountiful nature, that second mother, treats them as her spoilt children, and does all for them.   The forests abound with vegetables and exquisite fruits; the rivers, the lakes, and the ponds teem with fish; a few bamboos suffice to construct a house; while the periodical inundations render the lands wonderfully fertile. Man has but to sow and to plant; the sun saves him all further trouble; and he neither knows nor feels the want of all those articles of luxury which form part of the very existence of a European.

On the 13th November we arrived at a village called Arajik, where the land was more elevated. Here I killed several white squirrels, animals which I had not met with in the neighbourhood of Bangkok. It is only in the solitude and depth of the woods that one can fully admire and enter into the sort of harmony and concord which reigns in the songs of the various birds, forming such a pleasing kind of symphony that the voice of one is rarely overpowered by that of another; one can enjoy at once the general effect and the melodious note of the particular winged musician we prefer. Scarcely does the sun begin to gild the tops of the trees, when, alert and gay, they commence their morning hymn. The martins, the warblers, the drongos, and the dominicans, respond to the turtle-doves' cooing in the highest branches. Music of a less dulcet nature is discoursed by the aquatic and rapacious tribes, such as cranes, herons, and kingfishers, who from time to time utter their piercing cries.

I procured a guide in the mandarin of the village, who received me courteously, and offered me, in return for some trifling presents, a breakfast of rice, fish, and bananas. I requested his aid in arranging my purposed visit to Mount Phrabat, a favourite object of pilgrimage among the Siamese, who resort thither yearly in great numbers to adore the sacred footprint of Buddha. He volunteered to accompany me, an offer which I gratefully accepted.

The next morning, at seven o'clock, my host was waiting for me at the door, with elephants mounted by their drivers, and other attendants necessary for our expedition. At the same hour in the evening we reached our destination, and, before many minutes had elapsed, all the inhabitants were informed of our arrival; priests and mountaineers were all full of curiosity to look at the stranger. Among the principal people of the place I distributed some little presents, with which they were delighted; but my fire-arms and other weapons were especially the subject of admiration. I paid a visit to the prince of the mountain, who was detained at home by illness. He ordered breakfast for me; and, ex-pressing his regret at not being able to accompany me, sent four men to serve as guides and assistants. As a return for his kindness and urbanity I presented him with a small pistol, which he received with extreme gratification.

Drawn by M. Catenacci, from a Sketch by M. Mouhot.
ROCK AT THE SUMMIT OF MOUNT PHRABAT.

We proceeded afterwards to the western side of the
mountain, where is the famous temple containing the
footprint of Samona-Kodom, the Buddha of Indo-China.
I was filled with astonishment and admiration on arriving
at this point, and feel utterly incapable of describing the
spectacle which met my view.   What convulsion of

Nature—what force could have upheaved those immense rocks, piled one upon another in such fantastic forms? Beholding such a chaos, I could well understand how the imagination of this simple people, who are ignorant of the true God, should have here discovered signs of the marvellous, and traces of their false divinities. It was as if a second and recent Deluge had just abated; this sight alone was enough to recompense me for all my fatigues.

On the mountain summit, in the crevices of the rocks, in the valleys, in the caverns, all around, could be seen the footprints of animals, those of elephants and tigers being most strongly marked; but I am convinced that many of them were formed by antediluvian and unknown animals. All these creatures, according to the Siamese, formed the *cortège* of Buddha in his passage over the mountain.

As for the temple itself, there is nothing remarkable about it; it is like most of the pagodas in Siam—on the one hand unfinished, and on the other in a state of dilapidation; and it is built of brick, although both stone and marble abound at Phrabat. The approach to it is by a flight of large steps, and the walls are covered with little pieces of coloured glass, forming arabesques in great variety, which glitter in the sun with striking effect. The panels and cornices are gilt; but what chiefly attracts attention by the exquisite workmanship are the massive ebony doors, inlaid with mother-of-pearl of different colours, and arranged in beautiful designs.

The interior of the temple does not correspond with the
outside; the floor is covered with silver matting, and

H. CATENACCI. Del.

Drawn by M. Catenacci, from a Sketch by M. Mouhot.

RELICS FOUND ON MOUNT PHRABAT.

the walls bear traces of gilding, but they are blackene
by time and smoke. A catafalque rises in the centre,

surrounded with strips of gilded serge, and there is to
be seen the famous footprint of Buddha. To this sacred
spot the pilgrims bring their offerings, cut paper, cups,
dolls, and an immense number of toys, many of them
being wrought in gold and silver.

After staying a week on the mountain, and adding
many pretty and interesting objects to my collection,
our party returned to Arajik, the Prince of Phrabat
insisting on sending another guide with me, although
my friend the mandarin, with his attendants and elephants, had kindly remained to escort me back to his
village. There I again partook of his hospitality, and,
taking leave of him the day following, I resumed my
voyage up the river. Before night I arrived at Saraburi,
the chief town of the province of Pakpriau, and the residence of the governor.

Saraburi is a place of some extent, the population
consisting chiefly of Siamese, Chinese, and Laotian agriculturists; and consists, like all towns and villages in
Siam, of houses constructed of bamboo. They peep out,
half hidden among the foliage along the banks of the
river; beyond are rice-plantations, and, farther in the
background, extensive forests, inhabited solely by wild
animals.

On the morning of the 26th we passed Pakpriau,
near which the cataracts begin. The waters were still
high, and we had much trouble to fight against the
current. A little to the north of this town I met with
a poor family of Laotian Christians, of whom the good

PAGODA AT MOUNT PHRABAT, WHERE IS PRESERVED THE FOOTPRINT OF BUDDHA.

Drawn by M. Catenacci, from a Sketch by M. Mouhot.

Vol. I. p. 120.

Father Larmandy had spoken to me.* We moored our boat near their house, hoping that it would remain in safety while I explored the mountains in the neighbourhood, and visited Patawi, which is the resort of the Laotian pilgrims, as Phrabat is of the Siamese.

All the country from the banks of the river to the hills, a distance of about eight or nine miles, and the whole surface of this mountain range, is covered with brown iron-ore and aërolites; where they occur in the greatest abundance, vegetation is scanty and consists principally of bamboo, but it is rich and varied in those places where the detritus has formed a thicker surface of soil. The dense forests furnish gum and oil, which would be valuable for commerce if the indolent natives could be prevailed on to collect them. They are, however, infested with leopards, tigers, and tiger-cats. Two dogs and a pig were carried off from the immediate vicinity of the hut of the Christian guardians of our boat during our stay at Pakpriau; but the following day I had the pleasure of making the offending leopard pay for the robbery with his life, and his skin served me for a mat.

Where the soil is damp and sandy I found numerous traces of these animals, but those of the royal tiger are more uncommon. During the night the inhabitants dare not venture out of doors; but in the day-time the creatures, satisfied with the fruits of their predatory

---

* Father Larmandy was the interpreter of the Siamese embassy to France in 1860-1861.

rambles, skulk into their dens in the recesses of the
woods. One day I went to explore the eastern part of
the chain of Pakpriau, and, becoming excited in the
chase of a wild boar, we soon lost ourselves in the forest.
The animal made his way through the brushwood much
more easily than we could—encumbered as we were with
guns, hatchets, and boxes—and we ere long missed the
scent. By the terrified cries of the monkeys we knew we
could not be far from some tiger or leopard, doubtless,
like ourselves, in search of prey; and, as night was
drawing in, it became necessary to retrace our steps
homeward for fear of some disagreeeble adventure. With
all our efforts, however, we could not find the path. We
were far from the border of the forest, and were forced to
take up our abode in a tree, among the branches of which
we made a sort of hammock. On the following morning
we regained the river.

I endeavoured fruitlessly to obtain oxen or elephants
to carry our baggage with a view of exploring the
country, but all beasts of burden were in use for the
rice-harvest. I therefore left my boat and its contents
in charge of the Laotian family, and we set off, like
pilgrims, on foot for Patawi on a fine morning with a
somewhat cloudy sky, which recalled to me the pleasant
autumn days of my own country. My only companions
were Küe and my young Laotian guide. We followed
for three hours, through forests infested with wild beasts,
the road to Korat, and at last reached Patawi. As at
Phrabat, there is a bell, both at the foot of the mount

VIEW OF THE MOUNTAINS OF KORAT, TAKEN FROM PATAWI.   Drawn by M. Catenacci, from a Sketch by M. Mouhot.

and at the entrance of a long and wide avenue leading
to the pagoda, which the pilgrims ring on arriving, to
inform the good genii of their presence and bespeak a
favourable hearing to their prayers.   The mount is
isolated, and about 450 feet in height; its formation
is similar to that of Phrabat, but, although its appearance
is equally grand, it presents distinct points of variation.
Here are not to be seen those masses of rock, piled
one upon another, as if hurled by the giants in a
combat like that fabled of old.   Patawi seems to be
composed of one enormous rock, which rises almost
perpendicularly like a wall, excepting the centre portion,
which towards the south hangs over like a roof, projecting eighteen or twenty feet.   At the first glance
might be recognised the action of water upon a soil
originally clay.

There are many footprints similar to those of Phrabat,
and in several places are to be seen entire trunks of
trees in a state of petrifaction lying close to growing
individuals of the same species.   They have all the
appearance of having been just felled, and it is only on
testing their hardness with a hammer that one feels sure
of not being mistaken.   An ascent of several large stone
steps leads, on the left hand, to the pagoda, and, on the
right, to the residence of the Talapoins, or priests, who
are three in number,—a superior and two assistants,
appointed to watch and pay reverence to the precious
"rays" of Somanakodom.   Were the authors who have
written about Buddhism ignorant of the signification of

the word "ray" employed by the Buddhists? Now, in
the Siamese language, the same word which means "ray"
signifies also shadow, and it is through respect for their
deity that the first meaning is applied.

The priests were much surprised to see a "farang"
(foreigner) in their pagoda, but some trifling gifts soon
established me in their good graces. The superior was
particularly charmed with a magnet which I gave him,
and amused himself with it for a long time, uttering
cries of delighted admiration as he saw it attract and
pick up all the little pieces of metal which he placed
near it.

I went to the extreme north of the mount, where
some generous being has kindly had constructed, for the
shelter of travellers, a hall, such as is found in many
places near pagodas. The view here is indescribably
splendid, and I cannot pretend to do justice either with
pen or pencil to the grand scenes which here and
elsewhere were displayed before my eyes. I can but
seize the general effect and some of the details; all I can
promise to do is to introduce nothing which I have not
seen. Hitherto all the views I had seen in Siam had
been limited in extent, but here the beauty of the country
is exhibited in all its splendour. Beneath my feet was a
rich and velvety carpet of brilliant and varied colours;
an immense tract of forest, amidst which the fields of rice
and the unwooded spots appeared like little streaks of
green; beyond, the ground, rising gradually, swells into
hills of different elevations; farther still to the north and

east, in the form of a semicircle, is the mountain-chain of
Phrabat and that of the kingdom of Muang-Lôm ; and in
the extreme distance those of Korat, fully sixty miles
distant.   All these join one another, and are, in fact, but
a single range.   But how describe the varieties of form
among all these peaks !   In one place they seem to melt
into the vapoury rose-tints of the horizon, while nearer at
hand the peculiar structure and colour of the rocks bring
out more strongly the richness of the vegetation ; there,
again, are deep shadows vying with the deep blue of the
heaven above ; everywhere those brilliant sunny lights,
those delicate hues, those warm tones, which make the
tout ensemble perfectly enchanting.   The spectacle is one
which the eye of a painter can seize and revel in, but
which his brush, however skilful, can transfer most imperfectly to his canvas.

At the sight of this unexpected panorama a cry of
admiration burst simultaneously from all mouths.   Even
my poor companions, generally insensible to the beauties
of nature, experienced a moment of ecstacy at the
sublimity of the scene.   "Oh ! *di, di*" (beautiful), cried
my young Laotian guide ; and when I asked Küe what
he thought of it, "Oh ! master," he replied, in his mixed
jargon of Latin, English, and Siamese, " the Siamese see
Buddha on a stone, and do not see God in these grand
things.   I am pleased to have been to Patawi."

On the opposite side, viz. the south, the picture is
different.   Here is a vast plain, which extends from the
base of Patawi and the other mountains beyond Ayuthia,

whose high towers are visible in the distance, 120 miles off. At the first glance one distinguishes what was formerly the bed of the sea, this great plain having taken the place of an ancient gulf: proof of which is afforded by numerous marine shells, many of which I collected in a perfect state of preservation; while the rocks, with their footprints and fossil shells, are indicative of some great change at a still earlier period.

Every evening some of the good Laotian mountaineers came to see the "farang." These Laotians differ slightly from the Siamese: they are more slender, have the cheek-bones more prominent, and have also darker complexions. They wear their hair long, while the Siamese shave half of the head, leaving the hair to grow only on the top. They deserve praise for their intrepidity as hunters, if they have not that of warriors. Armed with a cutlass or bow—with which latter weapon they adroitly launch, to a distance of one hundred feet, balls of clay hardened in the sun, they wander about their vast forests, undismayed by the jaguars and tigers infesting them. The chase is their principal amusement, and, when they can procure a gun and a little Chinese powder, they track the wild boar, or, lying in wait for the tiger or the deer, perch themselves on a tree or in a little hut raised on bamboo stakes.

Their poverty borders on misery, but it mainly results from excessive indolence, for they will only cultivate just sufficient rice for their support; this done, they pass the rest of their time in sleep, lounging about the woods, or

LAOTIAN.

making excursions from one village to another, paying
visits to their friends on the way.

At Patawi I heard much of Korat, which is the capital
of the province of the same name, situated five days'
journey north-east of Pakpriau, that is about 120 miles;
and I determined, if possible, to visit it by and by. It
appears to be a rich country, producing, especially, silk
of good quality. Caoutchouc-trees abound, but are ne-
glected by the inhabitants, who are probably ignorant
of their value. I brought back a magnificent specimen
of the gum, which was much admired by the English
merchants at Bangkok. Living, according to report, is
fabulously cheap: six fowls may be purchased for a *fuang*
(37 centimes), 100 eggs for the same sum, and all other
things in proportion. But to get there one has to cross
the famous forest of "the King of the Fire," which is
visible from the top of Patawi, and it is only in the
dry season that it is safe to attempt this; during the
rains both the water and the atmosphere are fatally
pestilential. The superstitious Siamese do not dare to use
fire-arms there, from fear of attracting evil spirits who
would kill them.

During all the time I spent on the top of the mountain the chief priest was unremitting in his attentions to
me. He had my luggage carried into his own room,
gave me up his mats to add to mine, and in other ways
practised self-denial to make me as comfortable as was in
his power. The priests complain much of the cold in
the rainy season, and of the torrents which then rush

from the summit of the mountain; they are also greatly disturbed by the tigers, which, driven from the plains by the inundations, take refuge on the high ground, and carry away their dogs and fowls out of the very houses. But their visits are not confined to that period of the year. About ten o'clock on the second night of my stay the dogs suddenly began to utter plaintive howls. "A tiger! a tiger!" cried my Laotian, who was lying near me. I started up, seized my gun, and half-opened the door; but the profound darkness made it impossible to see anything, or to go out without uselessly exposing myself. I therefore contented myself with firing off my gun to frighten the creature. The next morning we found one of our dogs gone.

We scoured the neighbourhood for about a week, and then set off once more by water for Bangkok, as I wished to put my collections in order and send them off.

The places which two months previously had been deep in water were now dry; and everywhere, around their dwellings, the people were digging their gardens and beginning to plant vegetables. The horrible mosquitoes had reappeared in greater swarms than ever, and I pitied my poor servants, who, after rowing all day, could obtain no rest at night.

During the day, especially in the neighbourhood of Pakpriau, the heat was intense, the thermometer being ordinarily at 90° Fahrenheit (28° Reaumur) in the shade, and 140° Fahrenheit (49° Reaumur) in the sun. Luckily,

Drawn by M. Bocourt, from a Photograph.

SIAMESE NURSE AND BABY.

we had no longer to contend with the current, and our boat, though heavily laden, proceeded rapidly. We were about three hours' sail from Bangkok, when I perceived a couple of European boats, and in a room built for travellers near a pagoda I recognised three English captains of my acquaintance, one of whom had brought me to Singapore. They were, with their wives, enjoying a picnic, and, on seeing me, insisted on my joining them and partaking of the repast.

I reached Bangkok the same day, and was still uncertain as to a lodging, when M. Wilson, the courteous Danish Consul, came to me, and kindly offered the hospitality of his magnificent house.

I consider the part of the country which I had just passed through, extremely healthy, except, perhaps, during the rains. It appears that in this season the water, flowing down from the mountains and passing over a quantity of poisonous detritus, becomes impregnated with mineral substances, gives out pestilential miasmata, and causes the terrible jungle-fever, which, if it does not at once carry off the victim, leaves behind it years of suffering. My journey, as has been seen, took place at the end of the rainy season and when the floods were subsiding; some deleterious exhalations, doubtless, still escaped, and I saw several natives attacked with intermittent fever, but I had not had an hour's illness. Ought I to attribute this immunity to the regimen I observed and which had been strongly recommended to me— abstinence, all but total, from wine and spirits, and drinking only tea, never cold water? I think so; and I believe by such a course one is in no great danger.*

My intention now was to visit Cambodia, but for this purpose my little river-boat was of no use. The only way of going to Chantaboun was by embarking in one of the small Chinese junks or fishing-vessels, which I accordingly did on the 28th December, taking with me a new servant called Nion, a native of Annam, and who, having been brought up at the college of the Catholic priests at Bangkok, knew French well enough to be very useful to me as an interpreter. The boat was inconveniently small, and we were far from comfortable; for, besides myself and servant, there were on board two men, and two children about thirteen. I was much pleased with the picturesque aspect of all the little islands in the gulf; but our voyage was far longer than we expected, three days being its usual duration, while owing to a strong head-wind it occupied us for eight. We met with an accident which was fatal to one of our party, and might have been so to all of us. On the night of the 31st December our boat was making rapid way under the influence of a violent wind. I was seated on the little roof of leaves and interlaced bamboos which formed a sort of protection to me against the rain and cold night-air, bidding adieu to the departing year and welcoming in the new one; praying that it might be a fortunate one for me, and, above all, that it might be

---

* See the obituary notice.

PORT OF CHANTABOUN.

Drawn by M. Sabatier, from a Sketch by M. Mouhot.

Vol. I. p. 126.

The material originally positioned here is too large for reproduction in this reissue. A PDF can be downloaded from the web address given on page iv of this book, by clicking on 'Resources Available'.

full of blessings for all those dear to me. The night was dark; we were but two miles from land, and the mountains loomed black in the distance. The sea alone was brilliant with that phosphoric light so familiar to all voyagers on the deep. For a couple of hours we had been followed by two sharks, who left behind them a luminous and waving track. All was silent in our boat; nothing was to be heard but the wind whistling among the rigging and the rushing of the waves; and I felt at that midnight hour—alone, and far from all I loved—a sadness which I vainly tried to shake off, and a disquietude which I could not account for. Suddenly we felt a violent shock, immediately followed by a second, and then the vessel remained stationary. Every one cried out in alarm; the sailors rushed forward; in a moment the sail was furled and torches lighted, but, sad to say, one of our number did not answer to his name. One of the young boys, who had been asleep on deck, had been thrown into the sea by the shock. Uselessly we looked for the poor lad, whose body doubtless became the prey of the sharks. Fortunately for us, only one side of the boat had touched the rock, and it had then run aground on the sand; so that after getting it off we were able to anchor not far from the shore.

On the 3rd January, 1859, after having crossed the little gulf of Chantaboun, the sea being at the time very rough, we came in sight of the famous Lion rock, which stands out like the extremity of a cape at the entrance of this port. From a distance it resembles a lion couchant, and it is difficult to believe that Nature unassisted has formed this singular Colossus. The Siamese—a superstitious race—hold this stone in great veneration, as they do everything that appears to them extraordinary or marvellous. It is said that the captain of an English ship, once anchored in the port, seeing the lion, proposed to buy it, and that, on the governor of the place refusing the offer, he pitilessly fired all his guns at *the poor animal*. This has been recorded in Siamese verse, with a touching complaint against the cruelty of the Western barbarians.

THE LION ROCK AT THE ENTRANCE OF THE PORT OF CHANTABOUN.

Drawn by M. Sabatier, from a Sketch by M. Mouhot.

CHAPTER IV.

ON the 4th January, at eight o'clock in the morning, we arrived at the town of Chantaboun, which stands on the bank of the river, six or seven miles from the mountain range. The Christian Annamites form nearly a third of the population, the remainder being composed of Chinese merchants, and some heathen Annamites and Siamese. The Annamites are all fishers, who originally came from Cochin China to fish in the northern part of the Gulf of Siam, and settled at Chantaboun. Every day, while the cold weather lasts and the sea is not too rough, they cast their nets in the little bays on the coast, or in the sheltered water among the islands.

The commerce of this province is inconsiderable, compared with what it might be from its situation; but the numerous taxes, the grinding exactions of the chiefs, and the usury of the mandarins, added to the hateful system of slavery, keep the bulk of the people in a ruinous state of prostration. However, in spite of a scanty population, they manage to export to Bangkok a great quantity of pepper, chiefly cultivated by the Chinese at the foot of the mountains; a little sugar and coffee of superior quality; mats made of rushes, which meet with a ready sale in China; tobacco, great quantities of salted and dried fish, dried leeches, and tortoiseshell. Every Siamese subject, on attaining a certain height, has to pay to Government an impost or annual tribute equivalent to six ticals (eighteen francs). The Annamites of Chantaboun pay this in eagle-wood, and the Siamese in gamboge; the Chinese in gum-lac, every four years, and their tribute amounts to four ticals. At the close of the rainy season the Annamite Christians unite in parties of fifteen or twenty, and set out under the conduct of an experienced man, who heads the expedition, and indicates to the others the trees which contain the eagle-wood; for all are not equally skilled in distinguishing those which produce it; a degree of experience is requisite for this, which can only be acquired by time, and thus much useless and painful labour is avoided. Some remain in the mountains, others visit the large islands of Ko-Xang or Ko-Khut, situated south-east of Chantaboun. The eagle-wood is hard and speckled, and diffuses a powerful aromatic odour when burnt. It is used at the incremation of the bodies of princes and high dignitaries, which are previously kept in the coffins for a twelvemonth. The Siamese also employ it as a medicine. The wood of the tree which yields it—the *Aquilaria Agallocha* of Roxburgh—is white, and very soft; and the trunk must be cut down, or split in two, to find the eagle-wood,

which is in the interior. The Annamites make a kind
of secret of the indications by which they fix upon the
right trees, but the few instructions given me put me on
the right track. I had several cut down, and the result
of my observations was, that this substance is formed in
the cavities of the trees, and that as they grow older it
increases in quantity. Its presence may be pretty surely
ascertained by the peculiar odour emitted, and the hollow
sound given out on striking the trunk.

Most of the Chinese merchants are addicted to gambling,
and to the use of opium; but the Annamite Christians are
better conducted. The nature of these Annamites is very
different from that of the Siamese, who are an effeminate
and indolent race, but liberal and hospitable, simple-
minded, and without pride. The Annamites are short in
stature, and thin, lively, and active; they are choleric
and vindictive, and extremely proud; even among relations there is continual strife and jealousy. The poor
and the wretched meet with no commiseration, but great
respect is accorded to wealth. However, the attachment
of the Christians to their priests and missionaries is very
great, and they do not hesitate to expose themselves to
any dangers in their behalf. I must likewise own that,
in all my dealings with the pagan Annamites, whose
reverence for their ancestors induces them to hold fast
their idolatry, I experienced generosity and kindness
from them, both at Chantaboun and in the islands.

The missionaries at Bangkok having given me a letter
of introduction to their fellow-labourer at Chantaboun, I

had the pleasure of making acquaintance with the worthy man, who received me with great cordiality, and placed at my disposal a room in his modest habitâtion. The good Father has resided for more than twenty years at Chantaboun, with the Annamites whom he has baptized, content and happy amidst indigence and solitude. I found him, on my arrival, at the height of felicity: a new brick chapel, which had been for some time in course of construction, and the funds required for which had been saved out of his modest income, was rapidly progressing, and promised soon to replace the wooden building in which he then officiated. I passed sixteen days, very agreeably, with him, sometimes hunting on Mount Sabab, at other times making excursions on the rivers and canals. The country greatly resembles the province of Pakpriau, the plain being, perhaps, still more desert and uncultivated; but at the foot of the mountains, and in some of the delightful valleys, pepper is grown in some quantity by the Chinese.

I bought, for twenty-five ticals, a small boat to enable me to visit the isles of the gulf. The first I landed at was named Konam-sao; it is in the form of a cone, and nearly 250 metres* in height, but only two miles in circumference. Like all the other islands in this part of the gulf, it is of volcanic origin. The rocks which surround it make the access difficult; but the effect produced by the richness and bright green of the vege-

* A metre is equivalent to 3 feet 3¼ inches.

CHAPEL OF THE MISSION, CHANTABOUN.   Drawn by M. Sabatier, from a Sketch by M. Mouhot.

tation is charming. The dry season, so agreeable for
European travelling, from the freshness of the nights and
mornings, is in Siam a time of stagnation and death for
all nature; the birds fly to the neighbourhood of houses,
or to the banks of the rivers, which furnish them with
nourishment; rarely does their song come to enchant the
listener; and the fishing-eagle alone utters his hoarse
and piercing cry every time the wind changes. Ants
swarm everywhere, and appear to be, with the mosquitoes
and crickets, the only insects that have escaped destruction.

Nowhere did I find in these islands the slightest trace
of path or stream; and it was extremely difficult to
advance at all through the masses of wild vine and interwoven branches. I was forced to make my way, hatchet
in hand, and returned at night exhausted with the heat
and fatigue.

The greater portion of the rocks in the elevated parts
of these islands is elementary, and preserves traces of
their ancient deposit beneath the waters. They have,
however, undergone considerable volcanic changes, and
contain a number of veins and irregular deposits of the
class known as contact deposits that are formed near the
junction of stratified rocks with intruded igneous masses.

On the 26th we set sail for the first of the Ko-Man
islands, for there are three, situated close together, bearing
this name. The largest is only twelve miles from the
coast. Some fishing-eagles, a few black doves, and a
kind of white pigeon were the only winged creatures I

saw. Iguanas are numerous, and when in the evening they come out of their retreats, they make such a noise in walking heavily over the dead leaves and branches, that one might suppose it caused by animals of a much larger size.

Toward evening, the tide having fallen, I allowed my boat to ground on the mud, which I had remarked during the day to be like a peat-bog impregnated with volcanic matter; and during the whole night so strong a sulphureous odour escaped from it, that I imagined myself to be over a submarine volcano.

On the 28th we passed on to the second island, which is higher and more picturesque than the other. The rocks which surround it give it a magnificent effect, especially in a bright sunlight, when the tide is low. The isles of the Patates owe their name to the numerous wild tubers found there.

I passed several days at Cape Liaut, part of the time being occupied in exploring the many adjacent islands. It is the most exquisite part of the gulf, and will bear comparison, for its beauty, with the strait of Sunda, near the coast of Java. Two years ago, when the king visited Chantaboun, they built for him on the shore, at the extremity of the cape, a house and kiosk, and, in memory of the event, they also erected on the top of the mountain a small tower, from which a very extensive view may be enjoyed.

I also made acquaintance with Ko-Kram, the most beautiful and the largest of all the islands north of the

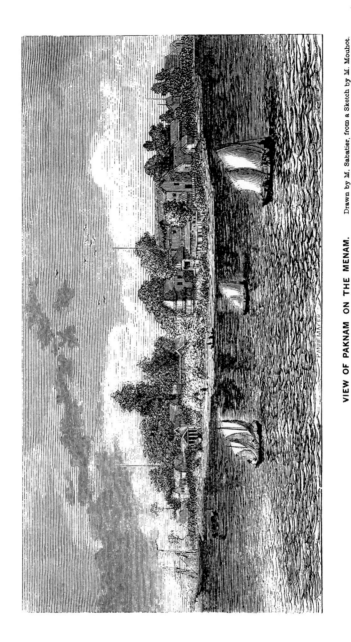

VIEW OF PAKNAM ON THE MENAM.　　Drawn by M. Sabatier, from a Sketch by M. Mouhot.

gulf between Bangkok and Chantaboun. The whole island consists of a wooded mountain-range, easy of access, and containing much oligist iron. On the morning of the 29th, at sunrise, the breeze lessened, and when we were about three miles from the strait which separates the isle of Arec from that of the " Cerfs," it ceased altogether. For the last half-hour we were indebted solely to our oars for the little progress made, being exposed to all the glare of a burning sun; and the atmosphere was heavy and suffocating. All of a sudden, to my great astonishment, the water began to be agitated, and our light boat was tossed about by the waves. I knew not what to think, and was seriously alarmed, when our pilot called out, " Look how the sea boils!" Turning in the direction indicated, I beheld the sea really in a state of ebullition, and very shortly afterwards an immense jet of water and steam, which lasted for several minutes, was thrown into the air. I had never before witnessed such a phenomenon, and was now no longer astonished at the powerful smell of sulphur which had nearly overpowered me in Ko-Man. It was really a submarine volcano, which burst out more than a mile from the place where we had anchored three days before.

On March 1st we reached Ven-Ven, at Paknam-Ven, the name of the place where the branches of the river unite. This river, whose width at the mouth is above three miles, is formed by the union of several streams flowing from the mountains, as well as by an auxiliary of

the Chantaboun river, which, serving as a canal, unites
these two places. Ascending the stream for fourteen or
fifteen miles, a large village is reached, called Bandiana,
but Paknam-Ven is only inhabited by five families of
Chinese fishermen.

Crocodiles are more numerous in the river at Paknam-
Ven than in that of Chantaboun. I continually saw them
throw themselves from the banks into the water; and it
has frequently happened that careless fishers, or persons
who have imprudently fallen asleep on the shore, have
become their prey, or have afterwards died of the wounds
inflicted by them. This latter has happened twice during
my stay here. It is amusing, however—for one is interested in observing the habits of animals all over the
world—to see the manner in which these creatures catch
the apes, which sometimes take a fancy to play with
them. Close to the bank lies the crocodile, his body in
the water, and only his capacious mouth above the
surface, ready to seize anything that may come within
reach. A troop of apes catch sight of him, seem to
consult together, approach little by little, and commence
their frolics, by turns actors and spectators. One of the
most active or most impudent jumps from branch to
branch till within a respectful distance of the crocodile,
when, hanging by one claw, and with the dexterity
peculiar to these animals, he advances and retires, now
giving his enemy a blow with his paw, at another time
only pretending to do so. The other apes, enjoying the

The material originally positioned here is too large for reproduction in this reissue. A PDF can be downloaded from the web address given on page iv of this book, by clicking on 'Resources Available'.

fun, evidently wish to take a part in it; but the other
branches being too high, they form a sort of chain by
laying hold of each other's paws, and thus swing back-
wards and forwards, while any one of them who comes
within reach of the crocodile torments him to the best of
his ability. Sometimes the terrible jaws suddenly close,
but not upon the audacious ape, who just escapes; then
there are cries of exultation from the tormentors, who
gambol about joyfully. Occasionally, however, the claw
is entrapped, and the victim dragged with the rapidity
of lightning beneath the water, when the whole troop
disperse, groaning and shrieking. The misadventure does
not, however, prevent their recommencing the game a few
days afterwards.

On the 4th I returned to Chantaboun from my excursions in the gulf, and resumed charge of my collections,
which, during my absence, I had left at the Custom-
house, and which, to my great satisfaction, had been
taken good care of. The tide was low, and we could not
go up to the town. The sea here is steadily receding
from the coast, and, if some remedy be not found, in a
few years the river will not be navigable even for boats.
Already the junks have some trouble in reaching Chantaboun even at high water. The inhabitants were fishing
for crabs and mussels on the sand-banks close to the
Custom-house, the *employés* in which were occupied in the
same pursuit. The chief official, who, probably hoping for
some small present, had come out to meet me, heard me

promise a supply of pins and needles to those who would
bring me shells, and encouraged his men to look for
them. In consequence, a large number were brought
me, which, to obtain otherwise, would have cost much
time and trouble.

CHAPTER V.

LIFE IN THE HILL-COUNTRY — MOUNT SABAT — HUNTING — TIGERS —SERPENTS —RICH VEGETATION OF CHANTABURI.

HERE I am, once more installed in the house of a good old Chinese, a pepper-planter, whose hospitality I enjoyed on my first visit to the place, two months ago. His name is Ihié-How, but in Siamese he is called Apait, which means *uncle*. He is a widower with two sons, the eldest eighteen, a good young man, lively, hardworking, brave, and persevering. He is already much attached to me, and is desirous of accompanying me to Cambodia. Born amidst the mountains, and naturally intelligent, there are none of the quadrupeds and few of the feathered tribes found in the district with whose habits he is not familiar. He fears neither tiger nor elephant. All this, added to his amiable disposition, made Phrai (that is his name) a real treasure to me.

Apait has also two brothers who have become Catholics, and have settled at Chantaboun in order to be near a Christian place of worship. He himself has never had any desire to change his religion, because he says if he did he must forget his deceased parents, for whom he frequently offers sacrifices. He is badly off, having incurred a debt of fifty ticals, for which he has to pay

ten as yearly interest, the rate in Siam being always
twenty or thirty per cent. Besides this he has various
taxes to pay—twelve ticals for his two sons, four for his
house, one for his furnace, one for his pig. The tax on
the pepper-field is eight ticals, one on his areca-trees,
one on the betel cultivated by him, and two *sellungs*
for a cocoa-tree; altogether thirty-nine ticals. His land
brings him in forty after all expenses are paid; what can
he do with the one remaining tical? The unlucky agriculturists of this kind, and they are many, live on vegetables, and on the rice which they obtain from the
Siamese in exchange for areca.

On my return from the islands, I had been detained
nearly ten days at Chantaboun, unable to walk; I had
cut my heel in climbing the rocks on the shore at Ko-
Man, and, as I was constantly barefooted in the salt water,
the wound soon closed. But afterwards I began to suffer
from it; my foot swelled, and I was obliged to re-open
the wound to extract a piece of shell which had remained
in it. As soon as I could leave Chantaboun I hired a
carriage and two buffaloes to take me to the mountain.
I experienced much gratification in finding myself again
amongst these quiet scenes, at once so lovely and so full
of grandeur. Here are valleys intersected by streams of
pure and limpid water; there, small plains, over which
are scattered the modest dwellings of the laborious
Chinese; while, a little in the distance, rises the mountain, with its imposing rocks, its grand trees, its torrents
and waterfalls.

We have already had some storms, for the rainy season
is approaching, vegetation is fresh, and nature animated;
the song of birds and the hum of insects are heard all
around. Apait has resigned to me his bed, if that can
be so styled, which consists merely of a few laths of areca
placed upon four stakes. I have extended my mat upon
this framework, and should enjoy uninterrupted sleep all
night were it not for the swarms of ants which frequently
disturb me by passing over my body, getting under my
clothes and into my beard, and, I almost fancy, would
end by dragging me out, if I did not from time to time
shake them off. Occasionally great spiders and other dis-
gusting creatures, crawling about under the roof, would
startle me by dropping suddenly on my face.

The heat now is quite endurable, the thermometer
generally marking 80° Fahr. in the morning, and 90° in
the middle of the day. The water of the streams is so
cool and refreshing, that a good morning and evening
ablution makes me comfortable for several hours, as well
as contributing to keep me in health.

Last evening Phrai, having gone along with my man
Niou to Chantaboun to buy provisions, brought back to
his father some Chinese bonbons, for which he had paid
half a fuang. The poor old man was delighted with
them, and this morning at daybreak he dressed himself
in his best clothes, on which I asked him what was going
to happen. He immediately began to clean a plank
which was fitted into the wall to serve as a sort of table
or altar. Above this was a drawing of a man dancing

and putting out his tongue, with claws on his feet and hands, and with the tail of an ape, intended to represent his father. He then filled three small cups with tea, put the bonbons in a fourth, and placed the whole upon the simple altar; finally, lighting two pieces of odoriferous wood, he began his devotions. It was a sacrifice to the manes of his parents, performed with the hope that their souls would come and taste the good things set before them.

At the entrance of Apait's garden, in front of his house, I had made a kind of shed with stakes and branches of trees, covered with a roof of leaves, where I dried and prepared my large specimens, such as the long-armed apes, kids, and horn-bills, as also my collections of insects. All this has attracted a crowd of inquisitive Siamese and Chinamen, who come to see the "farang" and admire his curiosities. We have just passed the Chinese New Year's-day, and, as there has been a fête for three days, all those living at any distance have profited by the opportunity to visit us. At times Apait's house and garden have been crowded with people in their holiday dresses, many of whom, seeing my instruments, my naturalist's case, and different preparations, took me for a great doctor, and begged for medicines.

Alas! my pretensions are not so high; however, I treat them on the "Raspail" system; and a little box of pomade or phial of sedative water will perhaps be represented in some European museum by an insect or shell brought to me by these worthy people in return for the good I would gladly do them.

It is very agreeable, after a fatiguing day's chase over hills and amongst dense forests, through which one must cut one's way axe in hand, to repose in the evening on the good Chinaman's bench in front of his house, shaded by bananas, cocoanut, and other trees. For the last four days a violent north wind, fresh in spite of the season, has been blowing without intermission, breaking asunder and tearing up by the roots some of the trees on the higher grounds. This is its farewell visit, for the south-east wind will now blow for many months.

This evening everything appeared to me more beautiful and agreeable than usual ; the stars shone brightly in the sky, the moon was clear. Sitting by Apait while his son played to me some Chinese airs on the bamboo flute, I thought to what a height of prosperity this province, even now one of the most interesting and flourishing in the country, might attain, were it wisely and intelligently governed, or if European colonists were to settle and develop its resources. Proximity to the sea, facility of communication, a rich soil, a healthy and propitious climate ; nothing is wanting to ensure success to an industrious and enterprising agriculturist.

The worthy old Apait has at last consented to allow his son to enter my service, provided I pay him thirty ticals, half a year's wages, in advance. This will enable him, if he can sell his house and pepper-field, to clear off his debt and retire to another part of the mountain. Phrai is delighted to attend me, and to run about the woods all day, and I am not less pleased with our bargain, for his knowledge of the country, his activity, his intelligence, and attachment to me, are invaluable.

The heat becomes greater and greater, the thermometer having risen to 102° Fahr. in the shade; thus hunting is now a painful, and sometimes impossible, exertion, anywhere except in the woods. A few days ago I took advantage of a short spell of cloudy, and consequently cooler weather, to visit a waterfall I had heard of in the almost desert district of Prion, twelve miles from Kombau. After reaching the last-named place, our course lay for about an hour and a half along a charming valley, nearly as smooth as a lawn, and as ornamental as a park. By and by entering a forest, we kept by the banks of a stream, which, shut in between two mountains and studded with blocks of granite, increases in size as you approach its source. Before long we arrived at the fall, which must be a fine spectacle in the rainy season. It then pours down from immense perpendicular rocks, forming as it were a circular peaked wall, nearly thirty metres in diameter, and twenty metres in height. The force of the torrent having been broken by the rocky bed into which it descends, there is another fall of ten feet; and, lower down, after a third fall of fifteen feet, it passes into an ample basin, which, like a mirror, reflects the trees and cliffs around. Even during the dry season the spring, then running from beneath enormous blocks of granite, flows in such abundance as to feed several streams.

I was astonished to see my two servants, heated by

their long walk, bathe in the cold water, and on my advising them to wait for a little, they replied that the natives were always accustomed to bathe when hot.

We all turned stone-cutters, that is to say, we set to work to detach the impression of an unknown animal from the surface of an immense mass of granite rising up out of one of the mountain torrents. A Chinese had in January demanded so exorbitant a sum for this, that I had abandoned the idea, intending to content myself with an impression in wax, but Phrai proposed to me to undertake the work, and by our joint labour it was soon accomplished. The Siamese do not much like my meddling with their rocks, and their superstition is also somewhat startled when I happen to kill a white ape, although when the animal is dead and skinned they are glad to obtain a cutlet or steak from it, for they attribute to the flesh of this creature great medicinal virtues.

The rainy season is drawing near, storms become more and more frequent, and the growling of the thunder is frightful. Insects are in greater numbers, and the ants, which are now looking out for a shelter, invade the dwellings, and are a perfect pest to my collections, not to speak of myself and my clothes. Several of my books and maps have been almost devoured in one night. Fortunately there are no mosquitoes, but to make up for this there is a small species of leech, which when it rains quits the streams and infests the woods, rendering an excursion there, if not impracticable, at all events very disagreeable. You have constantly to be pulling them off you by dozens, but, as some always escape observation, you are sure to return home covered with blood; often my white trousers are dyed as red as those of a French soldier.

The animals have now become scarcer, which in different ways is a great disappointment to all, for Phrai and Niou feasted sumptuously on the flesh of the apes, and made a profit by selling their gall to the Chinese doctors in Chantaboun. Hornbills also have turned wild, so we can find nothing to replenish our larder but an occasional kid. Large stags feed on the mountain, but one requires to watch all night to get within range of them. There are not many birds to be seen, neither quails, partridges, nor pheasants; and the few wild fowl which occasionally make their appearance are so difficult to shoot that it is waste both of time and ammunition to make the attempt.

In this part of the country the Siamese declare they cannot cultivate bananas on account of the elephants, which at certain times come down from the mountains and devour the leaves, of which they are very fond. The royal and other tigers abound here; every night they prowl about in the vicinity of the houses, and in the mornings we can see the print of their large claws in the sand and in the clay near streams. By day they retire to the mountain, where they lurk in close and inaccessible thickets. Now and then you may get near enough to one to have a shot at him, but generally, unless suffering from hunger, they fly at the approach of man. A few days ago I saw a young Chinese who had nineteen wounds on his body made by one of these animals; he was looking out from a tree about nine feet high, when the cries of a young kid, tied to another tree at a short distance, attracted a large tiger. The young man fired at it, but, though mortally wounded, the creature, collecting all his strength for a final spring, leaped on his enemy, seized him and pulled him down, tearing his flesh frightfully with teeth and claws as they rolled on the ground. Luckily for the unfortunate Chinese, it was a dying effort, and in a few moments more the tiger relaxed its hold and breathed its last.

In the mountains of Chantaboun, and not far from my present abode, precious stones of fine water occur. There is even at the east of the town an eminence, which they call "the mountain of precious stones;" and it would appear from the account of Mgr. Pallegoix that at one time they were abundant in that locality, since in about half an hour he picked up a handful, which is as much as now can be found in a twelvemonth, nor can they be purchased at any price.

It seems that I have seriously offended the poor Thaï * of Kombau by carrying away the footprints. I have met several natives who tell me they have broken arms, that they can no longer work, and will always henceforth be in poverty; and I find that I am considered to be answerable for this because I irritated the genius of the moun-

---

* The Siamese were formerly called Thaï.

tain.   Henceforth they will have a good excuse for idleness.

The Chinese have equally amused me.   They imagine that some treasure ought to be found beneath the foot-prints, and that the block which I have carried away must possess great medicinal virtues; so Apait and his friends have been rubbing the under part of the stone every morning against another piece of granite, and, collecting carefully the dust that fell from it, have mixed it with water and drunk it fasting, fully persuaded that it is a remedy against all ills.   Here they say that it is faith which cures; and it is certain that pills are often enough administered in the civilized West which have no more virtue than the granite powder swallowed by old Apait.

His uncle Thié-ou has disposed of his property for him for sixty ticals, so that, after paying off his debts, he will have left, including the sum I gave him for his son's services, forty ticals.   Here that is enough to make a man think himself rich to the end of his days: he can at times regale the souls of his parents with tea and bonbons, and live himself like a true country mandarin. Before leaving Kombau the old man secured me another lodging, for which I had to pay two ticals (six francs) a month, and I lost nothing in point of comfort by the change.   For " furnished apartments " I think the charge not unreasonable.   The list of furniture is as follows:— in the dining-room *nothing*, in the bed-room an old mat on a camp-bed.   However, this house is cleaner and larger than the other, and better protected from the weather: in the first the water came in in all directions. Then the camp-bed, which is a large one, affords a pleasant lounge after my hunting expeditions. Besides which advantages, my new landlord furnishes me with bananas and vegetables, for which I pay in game when the chase has been successful.

The fruit here is exquisite, particularly the mango, the mangusteen, the pine-apple, so fragrant and melting in the mouth, and, what is superior to anything I ever imagined or tasted, the famous "durian" or "dourion," which justly merits the title of king of fruits. But to enjoy it thoroughly one must have time to overcome the disgust at first inspired by its smell, which is so strong that I could not stay in the same place with it. On first tasting it I thought it like the flesh of some animal in a state of putrefaction, but after four or five trials I found the aroma exquisite. The *durian* is about two-thirds the size of a jacca, and like it is encased in a thick and prickly rind, which protects it from the teeth of squirrels and other nibblers; on opening it there are to be found ten cells, each containing a kernel larger than a date, and surrounded by a sort of white, or sometimes yellowish cream, which is most delicious. By an odd freak of nature, not only is there the first repugnance to it to overcome, but if you eat it often, though with ever so great moderation, you find yourself next day covered with blotches, as if attacked with measles, so heating is its nature. A *durian* picked is never good, for when fully ripe it falls of itself; when cut open it must be eaten at once, as it quickly spoils, but otherwise it will keep for three days. At Bangkok one of them costs one *sellung*; at Chantaboun nine may be obtained for the same sum.

I had come to the conclusion that there was little danger in traversing the woods here, and in our search for butterflies and other insects we often took no other arms than a hatchet and hunting-knife, while Niou had become so confident as to go by night with Phrai to lie in wait for stags. Our sense of security was, however, rudely shaken when one evening a panther rushed upon one of the dogs close to my door. The poor animal uttered a heartrending cry, which brought us all out, as well as our neighbours, each torch in hand. Finding themselves face to face with a panther, they in their turn raised their voices in loud screams; but it was too late for me to get my gun, for in a moment the beast was out of reach.

In a few weeks I must say farewell to these beautiful mountains, never, in all probability, to see them again, and I think of this with regret; I have been so happy here, and have so much enjoyed my hunting and my solitary walks in this comparatively temperate climate, after my sufferings from the heat and mosquitoes in my journey northwards.

Thanks to my nearness to the sea on the one side, and to the mountain region on the other, the period of the greatest heat passed away without my perceiving it; and

I was much surprised at receiving a few days ago a letter from Bangkok which stated that it had been hotter weather there than had been known for more than thirty years. Many of the European residents had been ill; yet I do not think the climate of Bangkok more unhealthy than that of other towns of Eastern Asia within the tropics. But no doubt the want of exercise, which is there almost impossible, induces illness in many cases.

A few days ago I made up my mind to penetrate into a grotto on Mount Sabab, half-way between Chantaboun and Kombau, so deep, I am told, that it extends to the top of the mountain. I set out, accompanied by Phrai and Niou, furnished with all that was necessary for our excursion. On reaching the entrance of the grotto we lighted our torches, and, after scaling a number of blocks of granite, began our march. Thousands of bats, roused by the lights, commenced flying round and round us, flapping our faces with their wings, and extinguishing our torches every minute. Phrai walked first, trying the ground with a lance which he held; but we had scarcely proceeded a hundred paces when he threw himself back upon me with every mark of terror, crying out, "A serpent! go back!" As he spoke I perceived an enormous boa about fifteen feet off, with erect head and open mouth, ready to dart upon him. My gun being loaded, one barrel with two bullets, the other with shot, I took aim and fired off both at once. We were immediately enveloped in a thick cloud of smoke, and could see nothing, but prudently beat an instant retreat. We waited anxiously for some time at the entrance of the grotto, prepared to do battle with our enemy should he present himself; but he did not appear. My guide now boldly lighted a torch, and, furnished with my gun reloaded and a long rope, went in again alone. We held one end of the rope, that at the least signal we might fly to his assistance. For some minutes, which appeared terribly long, our anxiety was extreme, but equally great were our relief and gratification when we saw him approach, drawing after him the rope, to which was attached an immense boa. The head of the reptile had been shattered by my fire, and his death had been instantaneous, but we sought to penetrate no farther into the grotto.

I had been told that the Siamese were about to celebrate a grand fête at a pagoda about three miles off, in honour of a superior priest who died last year, and whose remains were now to be burned according to the custom of the country. I went to see this singular ceremony, hoping to gain some information respecting the amusements of this people, and arrived at the place about eight in the morning, the time for breakfast, or "Kinkao" (rice-eating). Nearly two thousand Siamese of both sexes from Chantaboun and the surrounding villages, some in carriages and some on foot, were scattered over the ground in the neighbourhood of the pagoda. All wore new sashes and dresses of brilliant colours, and the effect of the various motley groups was most striking.

Under a vast roof of planks supported by columns,

SIAMESE ACTORS.

Drawn by M. Bocourt, from a Photograph.

forming a kind of shed, bordered by pieces of stuff
covered with grotesque· paintings representing men and
animals in the most extraordinary attitudes, was constructed an imitation rock of coloured pasteboard, on
which was placed a catafalque lavishly decorated with
gilding and carved work, and containing an urn in which
were the precious remains of the priest. Here and there
were arranged pieces of paper and stuff in the form of
flags. Outside the building was prepared the funeral pile,
and at some distance off a platform was erected for the
accommodation of a band of musicians, who played upon
different instruments of the country. Farther away some
women had established a market for the sale of fruit,
bonbons, and arrack, while in another quarter some
Chinamen and Siamese were performing, in a little
theatre run up for the occasion, scenes something in the
style of those exhibited by our strolling actors at fairs.
This fête, which lasted for three days, had nothing at all
in it of a funereal character. I had gone there hoping
to witness something new and remarkable, for these
peculiar rites are only celebrated in honour of sovereigns, nobles, and other persons of high standing; but I
had omitted to take into consideration the likelihood of
my being myself an object of curiosity to the crowd.
Scarcely, however, had I appeared in the pagoda, followed
by Phrai and Niou, when on all sides I heard the excla-
mation, "Farang! come and see the farang!" and immediately both Siamese and Chinamen left their bowls of
rice and pressed about me. I hoped that, once their

curiosity was gratified, they would leave me in peace, but instead of that the crowd grew thicker and thicker, and followed me wherever I went, so that at last it became almost unbearable, and all the more so as most of them were already drunk either with opium or arrack, many, indeed, with both. I quitted the pagoda and was glad to get into the fresh air again, but the respite was of short duration. Passing the entrance of a large hut temporarily built of planks, I saw some chiefs of provinces sitting at breakfast. The senior of the party advanced straight towards me, shook me by the hand, and begged me in a cordial and polite manner to enter; and I was glad to avail myself of his kind offer, and take refuge from the troublesome people. My hosts overwhelmed me with attentions, and forced upon me pastry, fruit, and bonbons; but the crowd who had followed me forced their way into the building, and hemmed us in on all sides; even the roof was covered with gazers. All of a sudden we heard the walls crack, and the whole of the back of the hut, yielding under the pressure, fell in, and people, priests, and chiefs tumbling one upon another, the scene of confusion was irresistibly comic. I profited by the opportunity to escape, swearing—though rather late in the day—that they should not catch me again.

I know not to what it is to be attributed, unless it be the pure air of the mountains and a more active life, but the mountaineers of Chantaboun appear a much finer race than the Siamese of the plain, more robust, and of a darker complexion. Their features, also, are more regular,

and I should imagine that they sprang rather from the
Arian than from the Mongolian race. They remind me
of the Siamese and Laotians whom I met with in the
mountains of Pakpriau.

Will the present movement of the nations of Europe
towards the East result in good by introducing into
these lands the blessings of our civilization? or shall we,
as blind instruments of boundless ambition, come hither
as a scourge, to add to their present miseries? Here
are millions of unhappy creatures in great poverty in the
midst of the richest and most fertile region imaginable;
bowing shamefully under a servile yoke made viler by
despotism and the most barbarous customs; living and
dying in utter ignorance of the only true God!

I quitted with regret these beautiful mountains, where
I had passed so many happy hours with the poor but
hospitable inhabitants. On the evening before and the
morning of my departure, all the people of the neighbourhood, Chinese and Siamese, came to say adieu, and offer
me presents of fruits, dried fish, fowls, tobacco, and rice
cooked in various ways with brown sugar, all in greater
quantities than I could possibly carry away. The farewells
of these good mountaineers were touching; they kissed
my hands and feet, and I confess that my eyes were not
dry. They accompanied me to a great distance, begging
me not to forget them, and to pay them another visit.

CHAPTER VI.

IMMEDIATELY on my return to Chantaboun, where I was again received with open arms by the good Abbé Raufaing, a French missionary associated as colleague with Father Larmandy, I began to collect information as to the best route to Battambong, the chief town of a province of the same name, which, above a century ago, was wrested from Cambodia by the Siamese. I made an agreement with some pagan Annamite fishermen to give them thirty ticals for taking me from Chantaboun to Komput, a province of Cambodia. The Annamite Christians demanded forty ticals, and provisions both going and returning. After taking leave of the abbé, who had shown me every possible kindness and attention on each of my visits, I embarked at noon, in spite of a heavy rain, as I wished to take advantage of a high tide. We arrived in the harbour at seven in the evening, and were detained there for two days by a contrary wind, too violent to allow us to leave without danger.

VIEW OF BATTAMBONG.

Vol. I. p. 171

Drawn by M. Sabatier, from a Sketch by M. Mouhot.

The material originally positioned here is too large for reproduction in this reissue. A PDF can be downloaded from the web address given on page iv of this book, by clicking on 'Resources Available'.

Two days later we reached Ko-Khut, where, again, pouring rain and a head wind compelled us to anchor about 100 metres from the shore in a small bay which was far from promising much security to our little craft. Our position was not agreeable; our frail bark, rudely tossed by the furious waves, seemed every moment in danger of being dashed upon the rocks. Our baggage, to which we had assigned the best place for preservation from wet, occupied three-fourths of the boat, and we were crowded five of us together in the bows, with no better shelter than some palm-leaves sewn together, through which the water dripped, and kept us continually soaked. The rain falling without intermission, we could not keep the fire alight to cook our rice, and for four days remained half-lying in the boat, scarcely able to move in the narrow space left for us, and our clothes clinging to us with wet. At last, on the fifth day, we had the pleasure of seeing the sky clear up and the wind change. About two o'clock in the afternoon, foreseeing a fine night, and having revived the drooping courage of my men by a stiff dose of arrack, we weighed anchor and left Ko-Khut with a fair breeze. It was quite a comfort to be able to move and breathe freely, and I spent a part of the night under my little awning of palm-leaves, enjoying the beauty of the heavens and the rapid movement of the vessel. At daybreak we perceived, about ten miles distant, the first of the islands of Koh-Kong. It is smaller than Koh-Chang, and neither so imposing in general appearance nor having such a splendid range of peaked hills. The island is nearly a desert, but it produces the beautiful cardamom, as also gamboge, collected from the bamboos, which the natives split open when hard.

I soon forgot the miseries of the first part of our voyage, and was amply recompensed by the shifting scenes of beauty presented to us by the group of islands we were passing. At length we reached the advanced posts of the pirates of Komput, from the heights of which they keep a look-out, and, as soon as a sail comes in sight, make preparations for an attack. We had no cause for fear, having no merchandise to tempt them; and, moreover, we were all well armed. About five in the evening we cast anchor in a little bay, where we cooked our rice, and my men lay down to take some repose, having had none the night previous. We were a day and a half's sail from Komput, and at midnight we resumed our voyage, gently rocked by the waves and favoured by a light breeze.

After passing the island of Phu-Quoc, which belongs to Cochin China, the view became more and more beautiful; land surrounded us on all sides, and we seemed to be sailing on a lake. The scenery in this gulf is truly enchanting. Eastward extend the coast and islands of Cochin China as far as Ita Jienne, and to the north and west are those of Cambodia, crowned by a mountain 900 metres in height, which is so like Sabab that Phrai called out to the pilot, "You are taking us back to Chantaboun; there is Mount Sabab." We were not,

Drawn by M. Bocourt, from a Sketch by M. Mouhot.

LEECH-FISHERS ON THE ISLE OF SAMET.

however, long permitted to enjoy the splendid picture
here displayed before us, for very shortly after our
entrance into the gulf large black clouds, gathering at
the summit of the mountain, by degrees hid it entirely
from view, the thunder growled, and a terrific wind arose,
which hurried our boat along at an extraordinary rate.
The pilot at the helm shook all over, and begged for
arrack to sustain his strength and courage. When the
storm had lasted half an hour a heavy rain began to
descend, and with it the wind moderated. We had now
arrived at the mouth of the river on which Komput is
situated.

It happened to be the day fixed for the King of Cambodia, then in Komput, to pass in review all the ships
lying in the roads; but for some time he had been
detained by the rough weather in a sort of apartment
erected for him on piles, in a place where the water was
shallow. As we passed the Custom-house, we perceived
the royal *cortége* advancing towards a large junk, which
his Majesty was having built as a trading-vessel for
Singapore.

The river leading to Komput is about 300 metres in
width, but, rising in the neighbouring mountains, its
course is but very limited. The magnificent tree called
by the Siamese Mai-Jakienne, and much prized by the
Chinese for furnishing masts for their junks, is found in
great abundance in the forests bordering its banks.
There are frequently six or seven ships loading at one
time in the roads, so that both Chinese and European

vessels may be constantly seen going up and down the stream.

Though Komput is now the only port of Cambodia, it is far from being as full of life and bustle as Bangkok, for the town boasts only 300 houses at most, and a population scarcely equal to that of Chantaboun. All its little commerce is supplied by Lower Cochin China, the ports of which are almost always closed against Europeans, so that rice, which is imported in a sort of contraband manner, some tons of gamboge, a little ivory, fish taken in the lake by the Annamites, a small quantity of cotton, and the valuable wood above mentioned, constitute the whole of the commerce of the town ; and I venture to predict that, when the ports of Annam are thrown open to Europeans, the Chinese merchants will abandon Komput altogether. And yet, under a better system of government, this country might supply a great number of articles, of which I will speak hereafter. It will not probably be long before what remains of this unfortunate land will fall under the dominion of some other power. Possibly, France has her eyes fixed upon it, with the view of annexing it to her possessions in Lower Cochin China.

The comparative exemption from heavy taxes and duties which the Cambodians enjoy, when compared with the Siamese, made me imagine I should be able to live here in comfort and abundance ; but I was disappointed. Almost every vice seemed prevalent at Komput—pride, insolence, cheating, cowardice, servility, excessive idleness,

are the attributes of this miserable people. It is often
remarked that no one should judge a country through
which he is merely a traveller, and that only those are
capable of doing so who have resided in it for some
time. I admit that, in the first case, one is liable to
make mistakes; but I state here what I see, and give my
impressions as I receive them, leaving it to more experienced travellers to correct me where I am in error.
Nevertheless, the first impression often proves ineffaceable,
and I may mention that frequently I have trusted less to
my own judgment than to the experience of others.

There are few travellers in Europe, America, or probably anywhere else, who have not had cause to complain
of the offensive manner in which custom-house officers
perform their duties, and often exceed them. In Europe
they earn their daily bread by annoying in every possible
way the unfortunates who are compelled, for the sake of
peace, to submit to their insolence and tyranny: here
they gain it by begging; they are licensed beggars. " A
little salt-fish, a little arrack, a little betel, if you please,"—
such are the petitions; and the more you give, the less
strict will the search be.

After having sailed up the pretty river for about a mile,
we came in sight of a house covered with creepers, and
surmounted by a cross, which indicated the residence of
the Abbé Hestrest, the head of the foreign mission here.
Reader, have you journeyed in foreign lands? Have you
ever for a time, more or less long, been separated from
vour friends and relatives—shut out from civilized

society? Have you been tossed about by tempests or buffeted by your fellow-men? Have you narrowly escaped some great danger? Have you been unhappy? Have you lost some one very dear to you? In one word, have you *suffered*? If you have, you will appreciate the feelings with which the solitary wanderer welcomes the divine cross, the heart-stirring emblem of his religion. It is to him a friend, a consoler, a father, a brother; at sight of it the soul expands, and the more you have suffered the better you will love it. You kneel down, you pray, you forget your griefs, and you feel that God is with you. This is what I did.

I had letters to the Abbé Hestrest from several of the missionaries in Siam. We therefore anchored, and I landed; but the nine days' inactivity to which I had been forced to submit had so cramped my limbs, that for a time I had almost lost the use of them, and could scarcely walk. The abbé received me like a brother, and offered me accommodation in his humble abode until I could find lodgings elsewhere. The first piece of news which he imparted to me was, that France was at war with Austria. I did not even know that there had been a difference between the two Governments.

Scarcely had I landed when the return of the king from his aquatic excursion was announced. The Abbé Hestrest conducted me to the banks of the river; and as soon as his Majesty perceived a stranger by the side of the priest, he gave orders to his rowers to approach the shore, and, when within hail, addressed the abbé:

" Who is the stranger with you ? "

" Sire, a Frenchman," replied my companion.

" A Frenchman ? " repeated the king, quickly.   Then turning to me, " You are French ? "

" Yes, sire," I answered, in Siamese.

" Monsieur comes from Paris," said the abbé; " but he has recently visited Siam."

" And what does he come to my kingdom for ? "

" He has a particular mission, which has nothing to do with politics; it is merely to see the country.   M. Mouhot will soon wait upon your majesty."

After a few minutes' silence, the king, waving his hand, and saying " *Au revoir,*" passed on.

I was at first afraid that the abbé had made me pass for a less humble and modest individual than I really was, and I should be forbidden the kingdom.   The very name of France is full of dread to these poor monarchs; and this present one lived in daily fear of seeing the French flag waving in the roads.   He is about sixty years of age, short and stout.   He wears his hair cut rather close, and his countenance is good-natured, mild, and intelligent.*

The king was reclining on a thick cushion in the stern of his boat, which was of European build.   Four rowers and a dozen young girls were with him; and among the

---

* Since M. Mouhot's journey, this king has died, and has been succeeded by his second son, a revolution in favour of the elder brother proving unsuccessful.

latter I remarked one, whose features were delicate and pretty, dressed in the European style, and wearing long hair. She would have been reckoned a pretty girl anywhere, and was, I fancy, the favourite, for she was in a richer costume than the others, and covered with jewels. She also occupied the place nearest the king, and seemed to pay great attention to her old adorer. The rest were fat, with bloated faces and vulgar features, and had their teeth blackened by betel and arrack. Besides a kind of petticoat, the corners of which are looped up and fastened to the sash behind, some wore a tight jacket, white or blue, buttoning over the chest; and had a red scarf, which, according to the custom of the Siamese and Cambodian women, was passed round the body under the arms, and tied at the bosom.

Behind the king's boat, in no apparent order, and at long intervals, followed those of several mandarins, who were not distinguished in any particular manner. One boat alone, manned by Chinese, and commanded by a fat man of the same nation, holding in his hand a halberd surmounted by a crescent, attracted my attention, as it headed the escort. This man was the famous Mun Suy, chief of the pirates, and a friend of the king. I was told that, two years before, he had been compelled, owing to some iniquities not very well known, to fly from Amoy, and had arrived at Komput with a hundred followers, adventurers and rovers of the sea like himself. After having remained there for some time, keeping the whole place in terror, and extorting by menaces all he

Drawn by M. Pelcoq, from a Sketch by M. Mouhot.

FAVOURITE WIFE OF THE KING OF CAMBODIA.

could from the market people, he conceived the project
of seizing upon and burning the town, and putting all the
inhabitants to the sword, intending then to retreat with
his spoils, if not strong enough to hold his ground.
Fortunately the plot was discovered, and the Cambodians from the neighbourhood were armed and assem-
bled in readiness to defend the place. Mun Suy, not
liking the aspect of affairs, embarked with his band in
his junk, and fell suddenly on Itatais. The market was
sacked in a minute; but the inhabitants, recovering
from their surprise, repulsed the pirates and drove them
back to their vessel with the loss of several men. Mun
Suy then returned to Komput, gained over by presents
first the governor· and afterwards the king himself, and
ever since has carried on his piratical acts with impunity,
making his name dreaded by all around. Loud complaints arose from the neighbouring countries, and the
king, either overawed by the pirate, or for protection
against the Annamites, appointed him commander of the
coast-guard.   Henceforth, therefore, he became a licensed
robber, and murder and rapine increased to such a
degree, that the King of Siam sent a naval expedition to
Komput to capture the malefactor and his gang. Two
only were taken and executed. As for their leader, he
was hidden, they say, in the palace.

Some days after my arrival I was installed in a house
built by the king's orders, and at his own expense, for
the accommodation of European merchants, who, however,
do not often visit Komput. Abbé Hestrest conducted me

through the city. The market-place, occupied chiefly by
the Chinese, is covered by a number of thatched huts
built of bamboo, in which are exhibited for sale, glass,
china, hatchets, knives, Chinese parasols, and other articles
of merchandise, native and foreign. The dealers in fish
and vegetables, and the Chinese *restaurateurs*, dispute
the street with pigs, hungry dogs, and children of all
ages and both sexes, in a state of nature, and dabbling
in the mud. Mingled with these are native women, re-
pulsively ugly, and effeminate and emaciated Chinamen,
with haggard cheeks, dragging themselves painfully along
to the opium-merchant's, the barber's, or some gambling-
house, three requisites to the very existence of a Chinese.
All the commerce is in their hands; and you meet ten
of them to one native.

I was introduced by the abbé at several Chinese
houses, where we were most politely received. The king
was expecting a visit from me, and had sent several
persons to find out who I was; his idea being, that I was
an officer of the French army in Cochin China, despatched
from thence to gain information about the country. I
begged M. Hestrest to accompany me to see the king;
for which purpose we proceeded a mile and a half up the
river to Kompong-Bay, which is the Cambodian part of
the town, and the residence of the governor, and where
his Majesty and suite were encamped.

When we arrived he was holding a kind of levée, in
a building constructed of bamboo with some elegance,
and covered with red cloth, but the interior of which

looked more like a theatre than a royal abode. Finding at the door neither sentinel nor porter, we entered without being announced. The king was seated on an old European chair, with two officers on each side of him, who from time to time offered him, kneeling, a lighted cigarette, or some betel, which they kept always ready. At a little distance stood his guards, some holding pikes ornamented at the top with white tufts; others with sheathed sabres in their hands. The ministers and mandarins knelt a few steps below his Majesty. On our entrance, chairs similar to the king's were placed for us close to him. Like his subjects, he generally wears nothing but the langouti, the native dress. His was composed of yellow silk, confined at the waist by a magnificent belt of gold studded with precious stones. At Cambodia, as at Siam, it is necessary to offer presents, if one desires to gain the royal favour. I had accordingly brought with me an English walking-stick gun, as a gift for the king. It at once attracted his notice.

"Pray show me that cane," he said, in Cambodian.

I gave it to him.

"Is it loaded?" asked he, seeing it was a fire-arm.

"No, sire."

He then begged for a cap and snapped it; unscrewed the barrel and examined it with great attention.

"If it would be agreeable to his Majesty," I said to M. Hestrest, "I shall be happy to offer it to the king."

The abbé interpreted my words.

" What did it cost?" asked the king.

" Sire, I dare not ask M. Mouhot. In Europe no one tells the price of what he gives."

The king then begged to look at my watch, and, after inspecting it attentively, again asked the price. The abbé then alluded to my design of visiting Udong, the capital of Cambodia, and of journeying through the country.

" Go to Udong; go about," said the king, laughing. " Very well." He then asked my name, and tried to write it; on which I drew out my pocket-book and gave him one of my cards. He seemed to wish for the pocket-book, and I presented him with it.

" Sire," said M. Hestrest, "as M. Mouhot is going to Udong, perhaps your Majesty will deign to facilitate his journey."

" Willingly. How many carriages do you want?"

" Three will be sufficient, sire."

" And for what day?"

" The day after to-morrow, sire."

" Take a note of that, and give orders about it," said the king to his secretary. He then rose, and, shaking hands with us, retired. We returned to our hotel. I say hotel, for it is the only lodging for strangers; and M. de Montigny, when ambassador at Komput, lived there, indications of which were afforded by the inscriptions scratched on the walls by the sailors belonging to the expedition, such as " Hotel of the king and ambassadors;" "Here is lodging for man, horse, and elephant gratis pro Deo;" "Good beds, sofas, and dining-tables on the floor;" "Sea-water bathing—in the river;" "Good table—in the market;" "Good wine—at Singapore;" "Nothing—for the servants."

CHAPTER VII.

ALL my preparations for departure having been completed, the Abbé Hestrest came on the morning of the day fixed, to invite me to breakfast with him; after which he offered to take me in his own boat to Kompong-Bay, where the promised vehicles were to meet us.

When we arrived there, none were to be seen. We applied to the first mandarin, who, chewing his betel, displayed his black teeth with a stupid grin, and I then perceived that I had been duped by these people, who are always and everywhere false; never yielding but to force, and holding the very name of a European in detestation. After various complaints, and remonstrances with the mandarins, we with great difficulty obtained three carriages, by courtesy so called; but the dog-cars in use in Holland would have been more serviceable to me; so I sent back the three wheelbarrows to the king, with my compliments, and hired other vehicles for myself.

Udong, the present capital of Cambodia, is situated north-east of Komput, and is four miles and a half from that arm of the Mekon which forms the great lake, lying about 135 miles from Komput as the crow flies. It is reckoned an eight-days' journey, travelling with oxen or buffaloes, and there are eight stations on the way. With elephants you can accomplish it in half the time; but only the king, the mandarins, and very wealthy persons can afford to keep these animals. The conveyances which I had engaged could scarcely hold my baggage, so that my men were obliged to make the journey on foot.

Perceiving in the shops several necklaces, bracelets, and rings formed of a material like jet, I inquired from whence it was procured, and was told that it came from the neighbouring island of Phû Quoc, where it was to be found in abundance. I afterwards handled a piece of this substance, and discovered it to be a sort of coal. It would burn well in a lamp, and greatly resembles the cannel coal of Scotland.

After traversing a marshy plain, where we knocked down several aquatic birds, we entered a beautiful forest, which stretches unbroken to the very gates of Udong. To cross this marsh I had to put on my hunting-boots, which I had not worn for some time, and consequently the leather had hardened so much, that, after two hours' walking in the heat of the day, the skin was rubbed off my feet in several places; and I was forced to take off the boots and continue my journey barefoot. Luckily, owing to the dry weather and the constant communication between Komput and the capital, the road was almost everywhere in good condition. The heat was intense, and our progress excessively slow; but at length we reached the first station, where I was lodged in a large hall, thatched and built of bamboo, which had been erected for the accommodation of the king and his suite. At night, guards were stationed at my door to protect me from robbery; and, thanks to the royal letter which I carried, I was respectfully treated. On the following morning I managed, at the cost of a franc of our money, to hire an elephant to take me as far as the next station.

From thence I continued my route barefoot, and our sufferings from the heat exceeded all I had ever imagined of the effect of the sun in the torrid zone. Its burning rays, falling on the sandy soil, became intolerable at ten o'clock in the morning, so that even the natives, the soles of whose feet were much harder than mine, could not bear contact with the bare ground, but sought for tufts of grass to step upon. The oxen could scarcely move, and showed every sign of pain and exhaustion; and, in spite of spurring and blows, often refused to stir. The water in the ponds was not warm, but literally hot; the whole atmosphere seemed on fire, and all nature languishing and prostrate. At ten o'clock we halted until three. We sadly felt the want of drinkable water, as also did our cattle, which suffered from thirst even more than ourselves. To make our tea and cook our rice, we had no resource but the stagnant pools, impregnated with unwholesome matter by the vomica-nuts which fall from the surrounding trees.

The day following I was fortunate enough to obtain another elephant; but after this there was no more help to be met with, and the greater part of the ensuing four days' journey I performed on foot, my attendants contriving to perch themselves on the corners of one of the waggons.   At this dry season a broad track in the middle of the road, which altogether is from twenty-five to thirty metres in width, is beaten hard by the frequent passage of vehicles and elephants, and the fine thick dust arising from it is very annoying. The remainder of the road is covered with grass and shrubs, and on either hand is the forest, with its trees tall, straight, and majestic, surmounted by immense tufts of leaves. The effect is that of a magnificent avenue; and from the regularity of the intervals between the trees, one might almost believe that it had been laid out by the hand of art.

The stations are equidistant from each other, about twelve miles apart; and at all of them, besides the old caravanserais for the shelter of ordinary travellers, new ones, much more spacious and ornamental, have been erected for the accommodation of the king.   There are also intermediate resting-places between every two stations, where travellers can obtain a welcome shelter from the midday heat.

On leaving Komput a low chain of hills came in sight on our left hand, but everywhere on our route we met with the same sandy soil, except in a single spot, which was stony, and contained veins of iron-ore. We passed

through but one village, and there, only, were a few
attempts at cultivation. In no other part of the forest
could I distinguish any traces of its being inhabited.
On approaching the capital, the prospect became more
diversified: we passed fields of rice, cottages encircled
by fruit-gardens, and country houses belonging to the
Cambodian aristocracy, who come here in the evening
for the sake of breathing a purer air than they can find
in the city. As we drew closer to the gates I found the
place to be protected by a large moat, surmounted by
a parapet, and enclosed by a palisade three metres
high. I expected to enter a fortified town, and, as my
countrymen were now engaged in giving a lesson to the
Cochin-Chinese, to be received by a sentinel with fixed
bayonet, and with the startling words, "You cannot
pass." But seeing no one, I pushed open the gate
and entered. It seemed that I was in the enclosure
surrounding the palace of the second king. The first
object that attracted my attention was a sort of cage,
something between a sentry-box and a pigeon-house, with
a small window at each of the four sides, intended for a
look-out house and signal-station in case of invasion. I
then found myself in the centre of a large square
surrounded by ramparts, and the access to which is by
two gates, one opening on the market-place, and the
other on the country. Within this walled space is, on
one side, the palace of the inferior king, and opposite
are the residence of a younger prince, his brother, and
a pagoda. All these buildings were thatched.

I hoped to find here, as at Komput, an "Hotel for the king and ambassadors," but, not seeing any sign hung out, I bent my steps to a house where many persons were passing in and out. It was the hall of justice, and the judges were then sitting. I sent my man Niou to ask if they would give shelter to a traveller, and had not long to wait for an answer, for both judges and accused came out to see me, and I was brought into the hall, where I was an object of great curiosity, all crowding round me and asking me what I sold.

The news of my arrival soon reached the ears of the king, and two pages were sent to request me to wait at once on his Majesty; but my luggage was not yet forthcoming, and I objected that I could not visit him in my travelling-dress. "Oh, that is nothing; the king has no dress at all, and he will be delighted to see you," was the reply. Scarcely had my waggons arrived when a chamberlain, followed by a page, came to say that the king was waiting for me. I went, therefore, to the palace, before the entrance of which were a dozen dismounted cannon, in whose mouths the sparrows had built their nests. Further off a crowd of vultures were devouring the remains from the table of the king and his courtiers. I was ushered into the audience-chamber, which communicates with his Majesty's private apartments, and is paved with large Chinese tiles, the walls being whitened with chalk. A number of Siamese pages, fine young men from twenty-five to thirty years of age, uniformly dressed in a langouti of red silk, were standing in groups, or seated in Oriental fashion, waiting the king's appearance. A few minutes after my arrival

Drawn by M. Janet Lange, from a Photograph.

PORTRAIT OF THE SECOND KING OF CAMBODIA
(NOW THE FIRST KING).

he entered, and every forehead was bowed to the ground. I rose, and he advanced towards me, with an air at once easy and distinguished.

"Sire," said I, "I had the honour of an interview with

the first King at Komput, and of being favoured by him
with permission to visit Udong."

"Are you French or English?" he asked, examining
me attentively.

"I am a Frenchman, Sire."

"You are not a merchant; why do you come to
Cambodia?"

"Sire, I came through Siam to see your country, and
to hunt here, if allowed."

"Very good.   You have been in Siam? I also have
visited Bangkok.   Come and see me again."

"As often as my presence will be agreeable to your
Majesty."

After a few more minutes' conversation, the king held
out to me his hand, which I kissed, and I then retired;
but had not proceeded far when several officials ran after
me, exclaiming, "The king is enchanted with you; he
wants to see you often."

The following day I devoted to making an investigation
of the city.   The houses are built of bamboos or planks,
and the market-place, occupied by the Chinese, is as dirty
as all the others of which I have made mention.   The
longest street, or rather the only one, is a mile in length;
and in the environs reside the agriculturists, as well as the
mandarins and other Government officers.   The entire
population numbers about 12,000 souls.

The many Cambodians living in the immediate vicinity,
and, still more, the number of chiefs who resort to Udong
for business or pleasure, or are passing through it on their

way from one province to another, contribute to give
animation to this capital.   Every moment I met mandarins, either borne in litters or on foot, followed by a

Drawn by M Sabatier, from a Sketch by M. Mouhot
CAMBODIAN CART.

crowd of slaves carrying various articles; some, yellow
or scarlet parasols, more or less large according to the

rank of the person; others, boxes with betel. I also encountered horsemen, mounted on pretty, spirited little animals, richly caparisoned and covered with bells, ambling along, while a troop of attendants, covered with dust and sweltering with heat, ran after them. Light carts, drawn by a couple of small oxen, trotting along rapidly and noisily, were here and there to be seen. Occasionally a large elephant passed majestically by. On this side were numerous processions to the pagoda, marching to the sound of music; there, again, was a band of ecclesiastics in single file, seeking alms, draped in their yellow cloaks, and with the holy vessels on their backs.

The third day after my arrival at Udong the court of justice was noisily opened at eight o'clock in the morning; and the loud voices of the judges and advocates were still resounding through the hall at five in the afternoon, having never for an instant been hushed, when suddenly two pages came out of the court of the palace, crying out, "The King!" A thunderbolt falling in the hall could not have caused a greater sensation than this announcement; there was a general hurryscurry; judges, advocates, accused, and spectators fled pell-mell, taking refuge in the corners with their faces to the ground. I laughed to see the legal functionaries, and the Chinamen with their long queues, rushing against each other in their eagerness to escape at the king's approach. His Majesty, who was on foot, now appeared at the entrance, followed by his pages. He waved his hand and called me to him. Immediately two attendants brought chairs and placed them on the grass opposite to each other. The king offered me one, and then entered into conversation with me, while the whole escort and every one near us remained prostrate on the ground; as far as the eye could reach, not a soul was standing.

"How do you like my city?"* asked the king.

"Sire, it is splendid, and presents an appearance such as I have never seen elsewhere."

"All the palaces and pagodas which you see from here have been built in one year since my return from Siam: in another year all will be finished. Formerly Cambodia was very extensive; but the Annamites have deprived us of many provinces."

"Sire, the time has arrived for you to retake them. The French are assailing them on one side; do you attack them on the other." His Majesty did not reply, but offered me a cigar, and inquired my age.

"I am twenty-three," he said to me. "I recognise you; you were at Siam with M. de Montigny."

"No, sire; your Majesty is mistaken. I have only been in Siam a twelvemonth."

I then sent for an elegant small Minié rifle, which the king's officers had examined in the morning, and presented it to him, asking him if he would deign to accept it. He desired me to load it, which I did. "It is done, sire," said I.

----

* The word *city* is here used to signify the royal palace, its appurtenances and fortifications.

" Is it possible ?   Fire, then."

He chose for a target a post some way off, and pointed out the place he wished me to hit.   I fired, and immediately his Majesty and the pages went to satisfy themselves that the aim was true.

" When do you wish to leave Udong ? "

" Sire, I should like to depart, the day after to-morrow, for Pinhalu and the other provinces."

" If you could remain one day longer, it would give me pleasure.   To-morrow you will dine with me ; on the day after I will take you to see the town of the first king, and in the evening we will have a play."

The play, I thought, will be curious, and therefore I decided to remain ; and, after I had thanked the king for his kindness to me, he shook hands with me, and we separated.   Evidently I was in high favour.   On the following morning messengers came from the king to place horses at my disposal, should I be inclined to ride ; but the heat was too great.   About four in the afternoon he again did me the honour of sending a horse to bring me to the palace.   I wore a white coat, vest, and trousers ; a helmet made of cork,* after the fashion of the ancient Romans, and covered with white muslin, completed my singular toilet.

I was introduced by the chamberlain into one of the

---

* A head-dress excessively light and cool, convenient, and shading the face and neck from the sun.   I strongly recommend it to travellers in hot countries.

king's private apartments, a pretty room furnished in the European style. His Majesty sat waiting for me, smoking, near a table covered with refreshments; and as soon as I entered he rose, and holding out his hand, and smiling, he begged me to sit down and begin my repast. I perceived that he intended, after the manner of the country, to do me honour by being present at the meal without partaking of it himself.

After introducing me, with much courtesy and friendliness, to his brother, a young man of fifteen, who was kneeling by his side, the king said, " I have had this fowl and duck cooked in the European fashion; tell me if they are to your taste."

All had been really exceedingly well prepared; the fish, particularly, was capital.

" Good brandy," said the king, in English (the only words he knew in that language), as he pointed to a bottle of cognac. " Drink," continued he.

The attendants then placed before me jellies and exquisitely preserved fruits, bananas, and excellent mangoes. Afterwards tea was served, of which the king also partook, having first offered me a Manilla cigar. He then wound up a musical-box, and put it on the table. The first air gave me great pleasure, all the more because I was unprepared to hear it in a royal palace. It was the *Marseillaise*. The king took my start and look of astonishment for admiration. " Do you know that air?" he asked.

" Yes, sire."

Then followed another scarcely less familiar, the air
of the Girondins, *Mourir pour la patrie.*

" Do you also know that ? "

As an answer, I accompanied the air with the words.
"Does your Majesty like this air ? " I inquired.

" Not so well as the first."

" Your Majesty is right; most European sovereigns
have the same taste."

" Napoleon, for instance ? "

" Napoleon, particularly."

My Annamite was with me, and filled the office of
interpreter, with a perfect tact which pleased the king.
The young prince now asked permission to retire, and
saluted his brother by bowing to the earth and raising
his clasped hands above his head. The king desired him
to return the next morning, and accompany us to the
palace of the first king; and the prince, passing out
into the courtyard, was lifted astride on the shoulders of
an attendant, and carried to his palace.

His Majesty then displayed to me his European
furniture, mahogany tables covered with china vases and
other ornaments of a commonplace description; above
all, he pointed out, as worthy of notice, two old looking-
glasses in gilt frames, a sofa, and various similar articles.
"I am but beginning," said he; "in a few years my
palace will be beautiful."

He afterwards took me into his garden, where were
some rare and curious plants, and a miniature artificial
rock. Then, on returning to the sitting-room, he con-

ducted me past the inmates of his seraglio, at least a hundred in number, whom curiosity had brought out to gaze at the stranger.

"You are the first foreigner who has ever been admitted here," he said to me. "In Cambodia, as in Siam, no one but the people on duty can penetrate into the king's private apartments."

I thanked him for the honour he had done me, and took leave. He told me to ask for all I wanted, and he would refuse no request. The only thing I desired was to have my journey facilitated; and to this end I begged him to furnish me with letters to the chiefs of the different provinces of his dominions, and one or two elephants. This he promised to do. This young sovereign is the presumptive heir to the crown. His father, who owes his throne to the King of Siam, is not permitted by that monarch to leave his own country; and as a guarantee of his fidelity, one or two of his sons have always been retained as hostages at the Siamese Court. It was thus that the young king passed many years at Bangkok, where, doubtless, he learnt the art of government, and whence he was not allowed to return to his own kingdom till it was apparent that he would prove a submissive and obedient tributary. Another brother, a prince of twenty-one, paid me a visit at night, unknown to his relatives, hoping to receive a present. He was very childish for his age, and wanted everything he saw; he was, however, gentle and amiable, and of superior manners.

The next morning the king sent for me at ten o'clock. I found him seated on a sofa in the reception-hall, giving

Drawn by M Janet Lange, from a Photograph.

A PAGE OF THE KING OF CAMBODIA.

orders to his pages about the order of march to be observed in going and returning. When all was ready, he entered a sedan-chair or palanquin magnificently carved and painted. His head and feet were bare, his hair cut in the Siamese fashion, and he wore a superb langouti of yellow silk, with a girdle of the same material, but of a lighter shade. The palanquin was borne on the shoulders of four attendants, and another held up an enormous red parasol with a gilt handle upwards of twelve feet long. The youngest prince, carrying the king's sabre, walked beside him; I was on the other side, and his Majesty often turned towards me to point out any striking object, and trying to read in my face what I thought of the effect produced on the people by his appearance. He sat in a careless attitude, one leg hanging out of the palanquin, and with his elbow resting on the morocco cushions.

At the approach of the procession all the collected population bowed themselves to the ground. In front marched three lictors, bearing in their hands bundles of rattans (the emblems of power); behind the palanquin came, two and two, the chamberlains and pages, numbering more than thirty, all dressed in red, and bearing on their shoulders pikes, sabres, or guns in cases. In this order we arrived at the outer entrance of the palace of the first king.

His Majesty here descended from his palanquin, and, still in the same order of march, we proceeded along an avenue about half a mile in length, planted with young trees, and bounded on either side by a wooden fence. The ground slopes gradually from hence, and is laid out in gardens and lawns, encircling which are a hundred little cottages with walls of clay and thatched roofs. "All these houses are inhabited by my father's wives; there is not a man in them," said the young king.

Farther on was a lake surrounded with rich and luxuriant verdure. On its banks, buried in foliage, which is reflected in the clear water, stands the royal residence, part of which is of bamboo, the rest being whitewashed. We went through several apartments, in which poor Annamite women were weaving silk, and, after passing in front of the treasury and the king's magazines, finally reached a vast hall which, here, is peculiarly called the palace. The interior does not come up to what might be expected from an outside view. It is stocked like a bazaar with glass bottles, vases filled with artificial flowers and covered by glass shades, cushions of all colours and sizes, boxes, slippers, old sofas, looking-glasses, washing-stands, and a variety of European articles, piled upon tables and shelves, and on the floor. As the young king was to spend the day at the palace, he now dismissed me, appointing one of his chamberlains to escort me home.

A little after sunset the people collected in crowds to witness the play which was to be performed on the king's return, expected at seven o'clock. The multitude was so dense that not a single inch of ground in the courtyard was unoccupied, and the walls, even, were all covered. At these festivities the people are apparently permitted to depart from the customary posture of humility, for every one was seated in Oriental fashion. The play was simply a phantasmagoria tolerably well managed, and accompanied by music more noisy than harmonious; but which appeared perfectly to satisfy the public.

Drawn by M. Bocourt, from a Photograph.

A NATIVE ACTRESS.

P 2

CHAPTER VIII.

ON the 2nd July, having taken our usual morning repast
of rice, we were ready to set off, and were only waiting
for the waggons and elephants promised me by the king.
They were not long in arriving, and we passed through
the city amidst an immense crowd of people who had
come from all quarters to witness our departure. We
were mounted on our elephants, and escorted by several
of the royal pages as far as the road to Pinhalú; all the
population prostrating themselves as before the king,
doubtless because he had paid me such marked attention.

We proceeded, at the rate of about three miles an hour,
on a good road, which was in some places raised more
than ten feet above the level of the wooded but marshy
plain which extends to the great arm of the Mekon.

Now and then we crossed handsome bridges built of
stone or wood, which certainly give a more favourable
idea of the state of engineering in Cambodia than in
Siam; for, even at Bangkok, the streams and canals are

spanned by thin, narrow planks, or by trunks of trees thrown across by the inhabitants, and not by the authorities.

About two kilometres from Udong is a sort of rampart formed of earth, in the form of a horseshoe. It environs a portion of the town, and was intended to defend the place in case of an invasion by the Annamites, an event which is yearly looked for at the time of the floods.

We met many pedestrians laden, probably, with provisions for the market. The road is bordered with miserable bamboo huts, like poultry-houses, raised on piles, which serve for dwellings for the unlucky Thiâmes, who were transported here by the king, a twelvemonth since, from the plains to the east of the Mekon, as a punishment for an attempted revolt which they were accused of.

We arrived early the same day at Pinhalú, a village of some size, situated on the right bank of the stream, many of the inhabitants of which are the descendants of Portuguese and Annamite refugees. It is the residence of a French bishop, Monsignor Miche, Vicar-apostolic of the mission to Cambodia and Laos. He was absent, but I found three good and benevolent missionaries, who begged me to wait for his return, and received me in that cordial and affectionate manner which is so pleasant to meet with in a strange land, and especially from fellow-countrymen. M. Fontaine, the eldest of the three, though still in the prime of life, had been a missionary for nearly twenty years. He was formerly attached to the

mission at Cochin China, and I had seen him on my visit
to Bangkok, where he remained some time before going
to Cambodia.   He was then feeble and suffering, but I
was glad now to find him stronger and full of animation.
I felt a true respect for this worthy man ; may there be
many labourers in the same vocation resembling him !

Drawn by M. Bocourt, from a Photograph

SIAMESE OF THE LOWER CLASS.

The second priest, M. Arnoux, was not only a fellow-
countryman, but our birthplaces were only distant from
each other a few leagues.   He was born in the depart-

ment of Russey, and I in that of Montbéliard (Doubs), so
that I had two reasons for being drawn towards him.
He belongs to the Cochin China mission, and had come
from among the savage Stiêns to renew his stock of
provisions; but, having been attacked by dysentery,
owing to the fatigue of the journey, he had been unable
to return. These two valiant soldiers of the Church, with
good and pure hearts, iron wills, and the energy and
courage of heroes, or, rather, of martyrs, had formerly
lived together, at a distant station, among the savage
Benous, and had suffered there terribly from fevers,
dysentery, scurvy, and other diseases. Among the fifty
Annamites who were with them in that refuge of Christianity, there frequently was not a single one able to
cook their rice, all being in the hospital. On hearing
these brave and worthy sons of our dear country describe
their past and present misery, I was sometimes as much
amused as affected, with so much liveliness was the narra-
tion given; but it is the characteristic of our dauntless
nation that her sons suffer and die gaily, and with smiles
on their lips.

Four days flew by rapidly in the society of these
friends, by whom I was detained till the return of their
bishop, whose acquaintance I much desired to make. I
knew that I should find in him a man of very superior
character; but I did not expect to find in this eminent
missionary a simplicity and humility equal to his talents
and strength of mind. Monsignor Miche is short and
slight; but under his frail exterior exist extraordinary

energy and endurance. The annals of the Cochin China
mission, as well as of that to Cambodia, must contain
many a page filled with the noble actions of this distinguished pioneer of Christianity, and with the persecution
and captivity he has suffered.   When a simple missionary,
he and one of his companions were imprisoned and beaten
with rods—a fearful punishment, which, at each blow, cut
open the flesh and made the blood flow.   They were
then conducted to their cells, in order that the torture
might be repeated on the following day, when their
wounds were beginning to heal, for the Annamites are
skilled in the refinements of cruelty.

"The suffering is dreadful," said his companion to
M. Miche; "I do not believe I can bear it a second
time."

"Be easy," he replied; "I will ask to receive your
blows for you." He did request this, and actually did
receive them.

Here the missionary is everything to the poor Christians,
physician to the body as well as the soul; and every day
he passes hours in listening to their disputes, and acting
as peacemaker.

The rule here is, that if a man cannot pay a debt, he
and his family become the slaves of the creditor. "You
are my slave," said a person to a young girl whom he met.

"How so?   I do not know you."

"Your father owed me money, and never paid me."

"I never knew my father; he died before I was born."

"Will you go to law?"

" Yes."

The man then consulted some mandarin, gave him
a present, promised him others, won his cause, and the
unfortunate girl, having no means to do the same, became
a slave.   It is the story of Appius and Virginia reproduced
in the East.   Corruption and barbarity are general in
Cambodia.

I now determined to visit the savage tribes living to
the east of the great river, 104° east long. from Paris,
and of whom I had heard M. Arnoux speak; he had promised me a welcome from M. Guilloux, the missionary
there.   I sent Niou back to Udong to ask the king for
the letter he had promised.   He soon returned with it
in due form, and on the 22nd July I quitted Pinhalú in
a small boat with two rowers, which I hired as far as
Pemptiélan, situated on the Mekon river, about forty
miles to the north of Pénom-Peuh.

Ever since I had been in Cambodia my servants had
been in a state of alarm, and it reached its height when
I informed them that we were about to set out on an
expedition to the savage tribes.   Cambodia is much
dreaded by the Siamese: and the mountains, and, still
more, the forests, inhabited by the Stiêns, have a reputation for unhealthiness, among both Cambodians and
Annamites, equal to that which, in France, is enjoyed by
Cayenne, whither condemned political offenders and male-
factors from the galleys are sent to die.   I doubt very
much if I could have met with any other men who would
have remained with me.

Drawn by M. Thérond, from a Photograph.

CHINESE MONUMENT AT BANGKOK.

On descending the great arm of the Mekon, which is here 1200 metres wide, I was astonished at seeing the current running from south to north instead of following the course of the river into which it falls. The banks of this river are peopled by the same race of Thiâmes whom I saw on my route from Udong to Pinhalú.

During more than five months of the year, the great lake of Cambodia, Touli-Sap, covers an immense space of ground: after that period there is a diminution in depth owing to the great evaporation, but its width remains nearly unaltered. Although its waters increase in volume during the rainy season, these are not swelled by the streams from the mountains on its western boundary, but by the strength of the current from the Mekon which pours into it its overflow.

As for the Malays, or Thiâmes, as the Cambodians call them, I made endeavours to investigate their origin, and also the traces which I supposed to exist in Cambodia of Israelite migrations. Monsignor Miche told me that he had never met with any Jews in the country, but that he had found, in one of the sacred books of the Cambodians, the judgment of Solomon exactly recorded, and attributed to one of their kings who had become a god, after having been, according to their ideas of metempsychosis, an ape, an elephant, &c.

The Thiâmes are the same as the ancient Tsiampois; but these Tsiampois, whence came they? What is the origin of this strange people, whom the conquests of the Annamites drove back, doubtless from the south of Cochin

China to Cambodia, but who form alliances with neither
of the races whose country they share, and who preserve their own language, manners, and religion? On
looking over the Life of the Abbé Gagelin, one of the
martyrs in Cochin China, written with talent and elo-
quence by the learned Abbé Jacquenet, I found what
I had long been in search of, and I extract the following
passage :—

"In the midst of Cochin China properly so called,
between the seas which surround it on all sides except
on the west, where it touches Cambodia, is the ancient
kingdom of Tsiampa. The inhabitants are a singular
race ; they never ally themselves with the Cochin Chinese,
their character, religion, and language raising insuperable
barriers between them. On submitting to the yoke of
the conqueror, the sovereign simply changed his title
from king to mandarin, but the constitution and ancient
laws remained in full vigour in his states, and he continued
to exercise absolute authority over his subjects.* It is
difficult for strangers to observe the domestic life of these
people; but it is said that they practise circumcision,
observe the Sabbath, abstain from the flesh of pork, and
offer the sacrifice of the red calf.† It is even said that
they possess the Pentateuch, but this I dare not affirm.
Strangely, however, all these observances, imitated no one

---

* This appears very doubtful, even to the missionaries in Cochin
China.

† M. Mouhot probably here refers to Numb. xix. 2.—*Tr.*

knows whence, are only vain ceremonies to these men,
enigmas to which they have lost the clue.   They have
not even retained a distinct idea of the true God; and
their worship, although mixed up with some of the rites
of the Mosaic law, is a real idolatry. One wonders whence
come this people. Are they an ancient colony of Ish-
maelites or Idumeans? Are they an offshoot of Judaism
thrown on to these shores? These questions are worthy
of consideration.   However it may be, their care to preserve their traditions pure from all alloy, and their
obstinate persistence in error, render them worthy of a
Jewish origin.   The Jews, in the days of their prosperity,
did not guard their faith more religiously than do these
people theirs in their new Palestine; and, in order to
avoid intercourse with strangers, and escape the prose-
lyting efforts of the missionaries, they have relinquished
to the Cochin Chinese all the advantages of the sea-
shore, and retired to the mountains and the interior of
the country.

" On the eve of the Assumption I bent my steps towards
the interior, to visit the Tsiampois, and find out whether
they would still reject the good news of salvation.   After
a few days' walking I arrived, I dare not say at one of
their towns, but at one of their principal dwelling-places.
These singular people have retained none of the power
ascribed to them by ancient tradition, according to which
they have held sway over Cambodia, Cochin China, Tong
King, and even Pegu, as far as the province of Canton.
Their governor has to pay a small tribute, but remains

as much ruler over his own people as before the conquest.

"I was anxious to find out the truth about their religion, but could only obtain scraps of tradition which a Christian could manage to put into form. One of these traditions teaches that the founder of their religion was a great man, a famous warrior, who worked marvels with a rod which is carefully preserved among them. I had the signal honour of being allowed to see it: it is about ten feet long, and is covered with a kind of red stuff, studded with yellow stars, having at one end an iron blade about an inch in length. With this rod in his hand, the founder of their faith controlled the elements, divided the waters, and calmed tempests; and it is pretended that this instrument still preserves its virtue of working miracles. They have, they say, a precious volume left them by this great chief. Their religious practices consist in the scrupulous observance of a seventh day of rest, in abstaining from certain food, especially pork, which they hold in abhorrence, and in the rite of circumcision which the male children undergo at the age of fifteen. When the girls arrive at the same age, the hair over the forehead is cut. They preserve a remembrance of certain days on which it was not lawful to work, nor even to leave their houses before sunset. Their prayers end with the word 'Amin,' much the same as the Amen of the Hebrews. They seem to have lost the idea of a Creator of heaven and earth, but worship the sky and the stars; there are, however, no idols in their temples. The priests who officiate there light candles on a table, burn incense, and, at certain times of the year, as in April and May, pass a month without going out of doors.   Clear away from this account," says the Abbé Jacquenet, " the mists of ages, and it is easy to recognise the traces of an Israelitish origin.   Comparing this with other missionary accounts, and the traces of these people found elsewhere, who will doubt that the torch of truth, which shone formerly between the great sea and Jordan, also shed its light over the extreme East?   Whether, to explain these facts, we consider the commercial relations of the Jews with these countries, particularly when, in the height of their power, the combined fleets of Solomon and Hiram went to seek the treasures of Ophir (a generic name used perhaps to designate the two Indies), or whether we come lower down, to the dispersion of the Ten Tribes, who, instead of returning from captivity, set out from the banks of the Euphrates and reached the shores of the ocean—whatever ground of explanation we resolve upon, the shining of the light of revelation in the far East is not the less incontestable.   Join to this light, those traditional truths carried with them as a sacred heritage by the families who were dispersed at Babel; and say what becomes of the extravagant praises lavished on Eastern wisdom by the sect of philosophers?   Passion and presumptuous ignorance joining hands tried to oppose wisdom from on high, and have left behind only a faint reflection of it."

CHAPTER IX.

We left Pinhalú at eleven, and by evening had reached the great bazaar of Cambodia, the distance being about eighteen miles. I had little to buy, for M. Miche and M. Arnoux had insisted on filling my boat with rice and dried fish, sufficient to last not only for my voyage but during the whole period I proposed to remain among the Stiêns.

I stopped a whole day to see the city, and make a few purchases of glass, brass wire, and cotton yarn, articles which would be useful as barter among the savages. The town is situated at the confluence of two great streams, and contains about 10,000 inhabitants, almost all Chinese ; but it has a floating population of more than double that number, composed of Cambodians and Cochin-Chinese, living in their boats. It was the time when most of the fishermen, returning from the great lake, stop at Penom-Peuh to sell part of their fish, and when a crowd of small merchants flock there to buy cotton, which is gathered in before the rains. Having traversed the city, which was long and dirty, I arrived at an eminence on which was built a pagoda, possessing neither beauty nor interest, but from whence there is an extensive view over a large tract of country.

On one side extend, like two long and wide ribands, across an immense wooded plain, the Mekon and its tributary; on the other, another plain and thick forest, bounded on the north-west and south by small chains of mountains.

Although the missionaries often pass through Penom-Peuh, my presence excited much curiosity among the people. The war in Cochin-China was the subject of all conversations, and in every one's thoughts. The reports of the Chinese and Annamites who had seen the taking of the town of Saigou were not flattering to the pride of a Frenchman. I had not seen the glorious bulletins of our Admiral, but had the pain of hearing our enemies stigmatise us as barbarians, and, describing the burning of the market, and the conduct of the soldiery towards defenceless women, speak of it as "the behaviour of savages." Thus the evil deeds of a less civilized ally were visited upon us, and our whole nation judged of by isolated acts, all but inevitable in time of war, especially in a country where the soldier suffers from the climate and privations of all kinds.

The people, perhaps the most corrupted in all the East, expected to find in us men superior, morally, as well as intellectually and physically; and I dare to flatter myself that before long they will learn to distinguish between the characters of the true French soldiers and their allies, and that in every respect we shall recover our ancient prestige.

The next day, descending the river toward the southern extremity of the city, we passed a floating town, composed of more than 500 boats, most of them of large size. They serve as an entrepôt for some merchants, and residences for others. All their money and the greater part of their merchandize is here kept, that, in case of alarm, they may be ready to take flight at a moment's warning.

Shortly afterwards we entered the Mekon, which was only now beginning to rise, as, throughout the country the drought had been excessive, lasting much longer than usual. This great river, the name of which signifies "Mother of Rivers," recalled to my mind the Menam, north of Bangkok, but its aspect is less gay; yet there is something very imposing in this expanse of water running with all the rapidity of a torrent. A few boats, scarcely distinguishable, toiled along: the banks, generally about 18 or 20 feet high, seemed almost deserted; and the forests were indistinctly discernible more than a mile beyond. In Siam the elegant foliage of the bamboos and palm-trees shows out strikingly against the blue sky, while the songs of the birds charm the ear: here, shoals of porpoises sail along with their noses to the wind, frequently bounding out of the water; pelicans sport on the margins of the stream, and herons and storks fly silently

THE RIVER MEKON AT PENOM-PEUH.   Drawn by M. Sabatier, from a Sketch by M. Mouhot.

from among the reeds at our approach. These are the sole objects of interest.

We passed the great island of Ko-Sutin, which is distant about 40 miles from Penom-Peuh, after five days' difficult and laborious travelling. The current was so strong that at every turn in the stream we were obliged, in addition to redoubling our efforts at the oars, to hold on by the reeds to prevent our being carried away.

The farther north we went the more rapidly the stream ran ; so that when the waters are high two miles a day are the usual rate of progress ; and it is a common occurrence for the boatmen to seek fuel for their evening fire in the same spot where they had cooked their rice in the morning.

About 25 or 30 leagues north of Ko-Sutin, on the confines of Laos, commence the rapids and cataracts : it is then necessary to leave the boats and take to pirogues, which, as well as the luggage, have often to be carried on men's backs. I made a halt of only a few hours, in order to see another voluntary exile, M. Cordier, a priest of great worth, from the Cambodian mission, who resides here.

I felt great compassion for this good man, on entering the chapel which he had built, and seeing the poverty and nakedness around. He came to meet me, and invited me to share his repast. For the last three years the poor missionary has been suffering from a dysentery, which has become chronic. However, he complains neither of his bad health nor of his poverty : the only thing that grieved him was the small number of converts he was called on to baptize, so deeply are the Cambodians attached to their idols.

"But you," said he to me; "do you know whither you are going? I am astonished that they allowed you to leave Pinhalú. Ask the Cambodians what they think of the forests of the Stiêns, and propose to some of them to accompany you: you would not find one. The rains have begun, and you are going to almost certain death, or will at least catch a fever, which will be followed by years of languor and suffering. I have had the jungle fever, and it is something terrible: even to the tips of my nails I felt a heat which I can only call infernal: sometimes an icy coldness would take its place: generally people sink under it: witness M. Lafitte, a young missionary, who a short time ago took the same journey; M. Comte, who died of exhaustion; and many others."

This account was not reassuring, nevertheless I had determined on my route: I knew that I should find there land and fresh-water shells whch I could find no-where else,* and that this tribe of almost unknown savages would afford me a curious and interesting study; and these considerations were sufficient to determine me to proceed. I trusted in God, and went on my way, M. Cordier's last words being, "May God be with the poor traveller!"

---

* Thence come the beautiful Bulimus Cambogiensis, Ptelin Cambo-giensis, and Ptelin Mouhoti.

Drawn by M. Sabatier, from a Sketch by M. Mouhot.

CAMBODIAN HUT AT PEMPTIELAN, ON THE MEKON.

Twelve miles higher up I left the river, and set off on my land journey at two o'clock in the afternoon, hoping to arrive the same day at Pemptiélan, a large village, where lived the mandarin to whom the king's letter was addressed. We did not, however, get there till eleven the next morning, having to pass the night at the foot of a tree, where we lighted a fire. I waited at once upon the mandarin, who is governor of the district, and he received me very well, in spite of the small value of the presents I made him, and immediately gave orders for waggons to be made ready for me. He then presented me with a quantity of tobacco and betel. His manners were, for a Cambodian, gentle and polished; and he questioned me much as to the war in Cochin-China, as well as about Europe, how long it took to get there, &c.

From the time we left Pemptiélan we had, except at rare intervals, to pass through dense forests, and at first the ground was so marshy that our miserable waggons occasionally sank deeply; and it required the united strength of the oxen and all our men to extricate them. We got over the latter part of our route more agreeably; for, as we reached a higher elevation, the ground became dry, and the aspect of the country more varied.

We had only been able to accomplish 60 miles in five days, and were still 30 miles from Brelum. I grew tired of the incivility of the inhabitants from whom I hired the oxen, and of the slowness of these animals: when we had no shelter for the night, we suffered much from rain and damp; our clothes were almost always soaked through;

and, to crown our misfortunes, my two servants were attacked with intermittent fever; the Annamite particularly, who had a tertian fever, lasting for ten days.

The mode of life of the Cambodians is similar to that of the Siamese : rice, as with the latter, is the chief part of their food : they eat it with vegetables, such as pumpkins or gourds, and wild potatoes. Those in better circumstances add to it fish, but rarely meat; and yet the country is as fertile as Lower Cochin-China, the soil of which yields so abundant a return for all that is put in the ground.

The poverty of the inhabitants of these miserable villages engenders a repulsive dirtiness : a strip of matting or an old filthy cushion thrown on the ground, and full of vermin, some basins of coarse Chinese porcelain, a sort of hatchet, and a piece of cotton, intended either for counterpane, scarf, or cloak, according to the season and time of day, are the usual contents of a Cambodian hut.*

We arrived at Pump-Ka-Daye, on the confines of Cambodia, and inhabited by about twenty Stiêns, who have approached the boundary in order to escape slavery in their own tribe. Our waggons halted before a small caravanserai, open to every wind; and after having carried in our luggage, our guides disappeared much faster than they had come. The chief soon presented himself, followed by some men : he had all the characteristics of a

---

* Cambodian is pronounced " Khmer," in the language of the country.

savage in his face, and of a Cambodian in his nature. I
handed him my letter, but he returned it, saying that he
could not read. " These, then," said I, " are the contents.
It is the king's order to all chiefs of villages where I
shall stop to furnish me with waggons to continue my
journey to Brelum." " We have no waggons," was the
answer.

We made ourselves as comfortable as we could till the
next day, when a second interview with the chief proved
to me that I should get no aid from him. I therefore
sent Niou with two Cambodians to carry a letter to
M. Guilloux, and bring me an answer. This arrived on
the evening of the fourth day ; and in it M. Guilloux
assured me of a cordial welcome, adding that he was
interested in my undertaking, and had already a great
regard for me, without seeing me, for my courage in
coming so far.* The good father sent me three waggons
from the mission settlement, and some of his Annamites,
as well as two Stiêns, to help me on my way. This letter
completely removed all fear of being a troublesome and
unwelcome guest to the poor hermit, and I set out
with pleasure and confidence. It took us two long days'
journey to reach Brelum : we encamped one night near
a torrent, lying on our mats beside a good fire, which we
lighted to keep off the ferocious denizens of these forests.
The second night we passed in a deserted cabin some
miles from Brelum ; and on the 16th August, at nine in

---

* See M. Guilloux's letter in the Appendix.

the morning, we came to a clearing of from 250 to 300
mètres square. We were betwixt two hills, at the foot of
which was marshy ground. On the slope of one I saw

Drawn by M. Sabatier, from a Sketch by M. Mouhot.

CAMBODIAN HOUSE.

two long bamboo houses, covered with thatch, and with
the mission-garden attached: higher up was the cross

planted two years before amidst these frightful solitudes
by the noble and courageous French missionaries.

Scarcely had we appeared when we were saluted by a
discharge of musketry. We replied as well as we could;
and while these sounds were reverberating among the
echoes of the forests, poor Father Guilloux, his legs
covered with bad wounds, which had confined him for
above six months to his mattrass, and which he had
received on the journeys undertaken through the prompt-
ings of his pious zeal, advanced with frail steps to meet
me along the tree-trunks thrown as a bridge across the
swamp. All honour to thee, noble son of our dear and
beautiful country!—thou who bravest poverty, privations,
fatigue, suffering, and even death, to bring to these
savages the blessings of religion and civilization! May
God recompense thee for thy painful and self-denying
labours, for men would be powerless to do so; thy reward
is not of this world. Besides, in these troublous and
warlike times, the virtues of the soldier are more appre-
ciated than thine. But continue thy divine work; intelligent eyes and hearts watch from afar; and if, in our
day, the military career is more honoured and better
recompensed than any other, there are still, be sure,
Christian hearts which feel it a duty to make known to
the world thy virtue and thy sufferings, thy privations,
and the benefits thou conferrest on these unfortunates.

CHAPTER X.

SOJOURN OF THREE MONTHS AMONG THE SAVAGE STIENS — MANNERS
OF THIS TRIBE — PRODUCTS OF THE COUNTRY — FAUNA — MANNERS
OF THE ANNAMITES.

I RESIDED nearly three months among the savage Stiêns.
Is this too short a period to enable me to form an
opinion of them? One would think so, on hearing
Father Guilloux repeat often that, although he has lived
here two years, he is yet far from knowing all their super-
stitions and *devilries*.

We are surrounded by forests, which are infested with
elephants, buffaloes, rhinoceros, tigers, and wild boars, and
the ground all about the pools is covered with their footprints. We live almost as in a besieged place, every
moment dreading some attack of the enemy, and keeping
our guns constantly loaded. Sometimes they come close
to our quarters, and we cannot go even a few steps into
the woods without hearing them. As a general rule,
however, they fly from the approach of man, and in order
to get a shot it is necessary to lie in wait either amongst
the branches of a tree or hidden amid the brushwood
near the spots where they come to drink.

Scorpions, centipedes, and, above all, serpents, were the
enemies we most dreaded, and against which precautions

were chiefly requisite; but the mosquitoes and the
leeches, though less dangerous, were the most troublesome and most inveterate plagues.   During the rainy
season you cannot be too much on your guard ; going
to bed or getting up, you are ever in peril of putting
hand or foot on some venomous snake.   I have killed
more than one in my house with a gun or a hatchet.   As
I write, I am obliged to be continually on the watch,
fearing to see one reappear on which I trod this evening,
but which made his exit without hurting me.   From
time to time, also, I stop to listen to the roaring of a
tiger, who is wandering round our dwelling and looking
longingly at the pigs through their fence of planks and
bamboos.   Again, I hear a rhinoceros breaking down the
bamboos which oppose his progress towards the brambles
encircling our garden, on which he intends to banquet.

The savage Stiêns who inhabit this region have probably the same origin as those who people the mountains
and the table-land which separate the kingdoms of Siam
and Cambodia from that of Annam, and which extend
along the great river from 11° north lat. and between
106° and 108° east long.   They form as many separate
communities as there are villages, and seem to be a race
distinct from all the people who surround them.   I am
myself inclined to believe them to be the aborigines of
the country, and to suppose that they have been driven
back from the sea and the rivers to the districts now
occupied by them by the successive invasions of the Thi-
betans, who have spread themselves over Laos, Siam, and

Drawn by M. Bocourt, from a Sketch by M. Mouhot.
SAVAGE STIEN.

Cambodia, and nothing that I can discover leads to any
other supposition.*

---

* The drawings of M. Mouhot at first sight recall those of the Poly-
nesians of the North, and more especially of the Carolinas, as they are
depicted in the works of Gutke, of Duperoy, and of Dumont d'Urville.

These savages are so strongly attached to their forests and mountains that to quit them seems almost like death, and those who are dragged as slaves to the neighbouring countries languish under captivity and try every method of escape, frequently with success. Like other savages, they have appeared formidable to their neighbours, and the fear inspired by them has occasioned exaggerated reports of their wonderful skill in shooting with the bow, as well as of the pestilential climate. However, it is a fact that fever prevails here terribly; numbers of Annamites and Cambodians have fallen victims to it, and I am assured that I am the only stranger who has come without suffering from it more or less. These people love the deep shade of the pathless woods, which they do not trouble themselves to cut down; but if they cling to their country, they do not to any particular locality, for if they meet with any inconvenience in their neighbourhood, or if any of their family die of fever, they raise their camp, take their children in baskets on their backs, and set off to make a settlement elsewhere; land is not wanting, and the forest everywhere alike.

These tribes are nearly independent, although the Cambodians on one side, and the Laotians and Annamites on the other, levy on the villages near them a triennial tribute of rice and wax. The King of Cambodia does not want the will to treat the Stiêns as he did the Thiâmes, in order to people some of his desert provinces.

The inscription placed—alas! so vainly—on our public edifices is here, notwithstanding slavery, the motto of the

R 2

Drawn by M. Bocourt, from a Sketch by M. Mouhot.
SAVAGE STIEN.

people, and its sincerity is evidenced in their practice. We use words; they act. If there is abundance at one house, the whole village shares in it, and when scarcity prevails, which is often the case, all alike suffer.

They work admirably in iron and ivory, and some tribes are noted, as in Annam, for their hatchets and the beautiful workmanship of their sabres. Their drinking-vessels are rude, but of their own manufacture, and the women weave and dye the long fine scarfs which they wear, the best of which are often valued at the price of an ox. They cultivate rice, maize, tobacco, various kinds of vegetables, and fruit-trees, such as bananas, mangoes, and oranges. Every person of any substance possesses several

slaves, and a field, always at some distance from the
village, and very carefully attended to. In these fields, in
little huts raised on piles, the Stiêns pass the whole of
the rainy season, during which they can neither hunt
nor fish, both on account of the inclement weather and
the leeches, the immense numbers of which, as in the
forests of Siam, make them a perfect pest.

Their manner of preparing a rice-field is very different
from the way in which our agriculturists set about
matters. As soon as the first rains begin to fall, the
Stiên chooses his ground, and busies himself in clearing
it. This would be a laborious task for a European; but
he, with his hatchet with cane handle, has in a few days
cut down a thicket of bamboos 100 or 150 mètres square.
If he meets with any tree too large for him to manage,
he leaves it standing. After a few days, when the canes
are a little dry, he sets fire to them, and the field is
soon cleared. As for the roots, he cares little about
them, as no digging is required; on this virgin soil everything grows with little labour. There only remains to sow
the seed, and for this purpose he takes two long bamboos,
which he lays in a line on the ground; then, with a
stick in each hand, he makes on each side of this line
holes about an inch or an inch and a half deep at short
distances. The man's work is now finished, and that of
the woman begins: stooping down, she follows the line
traced by her husband, and from a basket carried at her
left side takes a handful of rice, of which she throws a
few grains into each hole with great rapidity, and at the

same time so dexterously that it is rare for any to fall outside. In a few hours the task is finished, for here there is no need of harrow or plough; kind Nature will soon send some violent showers, which, washing the soil over the holes, will cover the seeds. Then the proprietor establishes himself in his hut, where, as he smokes his cigarette (made of tobacco rolled in some leaf), he lets fly his arrows at the wild boars, apes, or goats, or amuses himself by frightening away the doves and parroquets. To this end, a couple of bamboos are so placed in the middle of the field that, by pulling a rope made of rattan, they are made to strike against each other, and the noise scares away the birds, which without some such contrivance would eat up all the seed. The harvest is reaped at the end of October. Generally, two months previously poverty and famine begin to make themselves felt. As long as provisions last they feast without ever thinking of the morrow; when they are exhausted they are reduced to eat serpents, toads, and bats, which last are found in great numbers in the hollows of the old bamboos. Often they have even to content themselves with the seeds of the maize, young bamboo-shoots, wild roots, and other spontaneous productions of the ground.

All the domestic animals of the neighbouring countries, such as oxen, pigs, fowls, and ducks, are found here, but in small numbers. Elephants are scarce; but farther north, among the tribe of the Benams, it is said that no village is without them.

When the harvest has been gathered in the Stiêns

L. SARGENT. SC

E. BOCOURT.

SAVAGE STIENS SOWING THEIR RICE.

Drawn by M. Bocourt, from a Sketch by M. Mouhot.

commence a series of festivities. The rice having been
piled up in oblong stacks, they take from these every
morning as much as suffices for the day's consumption.
One community sends invitations to another, and the
inhabitants of a wealthy village will often kill as many as
ten oxen for the entertainment; all must be consumed
before they separate, and day and night they eat and
drink to the accompaniment of the Chinese tam-tam and
tambourine. This excess, after a long period of privation,
brings on illness, commonly the itch and other cutaneous
disorders. Much of this, however, also proceeds from the
want of salt, which they cannot always procure. For
all internal complaints, the general remedy here, as in
Cambodia, is an iron heated in the fire and applied to the
pit of the stomach, and there are few men without scars
on this part of the body.

They are acquainted with many of the remedies drawn
from simples; they never cover up a wound or sore, but
leave it exposed to the air and sun, and it generally heals.
They appear to be exempt from leprosy, so common
among the Chinese; but then they are very cleanly, and
bathe in all weathers, often three times a day.

The Stiêns have no resemblance to either the Cambodian or Annamite races; like the last, however, they
wear the hair long, twisted up, and fastened by a bamboo
comb, in which is often inserted, for ornament, a piece of
brass wire surmounted by the crest of a pheasant. They
are usually above the middle height, are well proportioned
and robust; their features are regular, and the thick

eyebrows and beard of the men, when they do not pull out the hair from the face, give them a grave appearance. The forehead is well developed, and announces an intelligence much beyond that of the Annamites. Their manners are hospitable, and a stranger is always certain of being well received and feasted. They either kill a pig or fowl, and offer you wine, which is not drunk out of any sort of vessel, but sucked, through a bamboo cane, from a large jar; it is made from rice, fermented, but rarely distilled. To refuse a pipe when offered is considered a great rudeness, which more than one savage has paid for by a knife-thrust. It is also etiquette to eat the whole of the food set before you.

Their only dress is the long scarf I have already mentioned, and which, when worn, appears only about two inches wide. I often surprised them quite naked in their cabins; but on perceiving me they always covered themselves.

The greatest liberty is allowed to slaves, and corporal punishment is never inflicted on any one. For theft, a forfeit is exacted of a pig or ox, and several jars of wine, of which the whole village partake. If the fine be not paid, it rapidly increases in amount; the offender is soon in debt to the community for fifteen or twenty buffaloes, and finally he is sold as a slave.

The Stiêns have neither priests nor temples, yet they recognise the existence of a supreme being, to whom they refer everything good or evil; they call him "Brâ," and invoke him in all cases. They believe also in an evil genius, and attribute all diseases to him. If any one be suffering from illness, they say it is the demon tormenting him; and, with this idea, make, night and day, an insupportable noise around the patient, which they keep up until one of the party falls in a kind of fit, crying out, "He has passed into my body; he is stifling me." They then question the new patient, asking him, first, what remedies to give the sick man, and how the demon can be made to abandon his prey. Sometimes the sacrifice of a pig or an ox is required, often a human victim; in this latter case they pitilessly seize upon a slave and offer him up to the evil genius.

Funerals are solemnly performed, the whole village assisting, with the exception of the nearest relatives, who generally remain at home. All those present fill the air with lamentable cries. They bury their dead near their dwellings, covering the tomb with a little roof of branches, beneath which they place gourds full of water, and sometimes small bows and arrows; and every day some member of the family comes and sows a few grains of rice, that the dead may have something to eat. These customs resemble those of the Chinese.

Before every meal they take care to spill a little rice to feed the souls of their ancestors, and in their fields and other places formerly frequented by them they make similar little offerings to them. At the end of a long bamboo planted in the ground they suspend plumes of reeds; lower down are fastened smaller bamboos containing a few drops of wine or water; and, lastly, on a slight trellis-work raised above the ground, is laid some earth, in which they stick an arrow, and on which they throw a few grains of cooked rice, a bone, a little tobacco, and a leaf.

According to their belief, animals also have souls which wander about after their death; thus, when they have killed one, fearing lest its soul should come and torment them, they ask pardon for the evil they have done to it, and offer sacrifices proportioned to the strength and size of the animal.   For an elephant, the ceremony is conducted with pomp; the head is ornamented with crowns, and musical performances on the tam-tam and tambourine, with singing, are continued for seven consecutive days. The whole village, summoned by sound of trumpet, assembles to take part in the fête, and every one is entitled to a portion of the flesh.

The Stiêns smoke the flesh of the animals when they desire to preserve it for any length of time; but ordinarily, all those taken in the chase are eaten on the spot, and within a few days; they then merely singe them whole, without skinning, and afterwards cut them in pieces and cook them.

It is rare to meet a Stiên without his cross-bow in his hand, his knife over his shoulder, and a basket on his back, which serves both for quiver and game-bag. Hunting and fishing occupy all the time not given to the cultivation of the ground.   They are indefatigable in the chase, and glide amidst the thickest woods with the speed of a deer, seeming not to feel fatigue.   The women appear as robust and strong as the men. Their cross-bows are very effective weapons, and they are skilful in the use of them; but rarely shoot from a distance of more than fifty paces. They use poisoned arrows for the larger animals, the venom being extremely rapid in its effects; if the beast, whether it be elephant, tiger, or rhinoceros, have the skin ever so slightly pierced, so that the poison touches the blood, it is almost certain to be found dead a few hundred yards from the place where it was struck.

They are very fond of ornaments, particularly beads of brilliant colours, which they make into bracelets. Glass ornaments and brass wire pass among them as money; a buffalo or an ox is valued at six armfulls of thick brass wire; a pig is nearly as dear; but for a small piece of fine wire or a bead necklace you can purchase a pheasant or a hundred ears of maize. Men generally wear a bracelet above the elbow and one at the wrist; but the women cover both arms and legs with these ornaments. Both sexes have their ears pierced, and widen the hole every year by inserting pieces of bone or ivory three inches long.

Polygamy is held in honour among the Stiêns, although only the chiefs are rich enough to allow themselves the luxury of several wives.

While I was among them there was a total eclipse of the sun, which, if I remember right, was also visible in England. Like the Cambodians, on the occurrence of such phenomena, they believe that some being has swallowed up the sun and moon; and in order to deliver them, they made a frightful noise, beat the tam-tam, uttered savage cries, and shot arrows into the air, until the sun re-appeared.

One of their favourite amusements is to send up kites, to which they attach a musical instrument somewhat resembling a bow, and this, when agitated by the wind, produces sweet and melodious sounds to which they are fond of listening.

Their memories are bad, and they have great difficulty in learning to calculate. If a hundred ears of maize are to be offered for sale, they are arranged in tens, to make sure that the number is correct. Their notions of geography are very limited; they imagine that white men inhabit only a few obscure corners of the globe, and, judging of them by the Catholic missionaries, doubt much if they have any women among them.

Hostilities between one village and another are not infrequent, but they are never very serious: they seek to surprise and take one another prisoners in the fields or pathways, and the captives are sold as slaves to the Laotians or Cambodians. Their disposition is gentle and timid, and at the least alarm of an enemy they retire into the forest, previously placing in the paths sharp-pointed stakes of bamboo, which often pierce quite through the feet of their pursuers.

The manners of the savages of Brelum and those of the surrounding villages differ considerably; this is owing to the influence of the good and courageous missionaries, who, although they do not make many converts—which

is their chief trouble—have at least the consolation of
being able by their presence, good counsel, and example,
to soften and enlighten these poor creatures—in one word,
to civilize them.

The Fauna of this country does not differ much from
that of the kingdom of Siam; thus, with the exception
of some beautiful new species of insects and land shells,
and a number of interesting birds, I shall gain by my
excursion nothing but the pleasure of having been able
to study the habits of a curious people, and the not inferior
gratification of making them known to the public, should
these rough notes, written hastily, and with no claim to
any merit but truth, be destined to see the light. Whether
God reserves for me the happiness of again seeing my
native country, in which event it will be my endeavour
to put them into some sort of readable shape; or whether
I fall a victim to pestilence or ferocious beasts, and some
kind person takes charge of these sheets, scribbled
generally by the light of a torch, and on my knees at the
foot of a tree, amidst interruptions of all sorts, of which
the mosquitoes are not the least annoying; in either case,
living or dead, I shall need, I am aware, an indulgence
seldom granted.   Most readers prefer being amused to
being instructed; while my sole aim has been to paint
faithfully, and to the best of my poor abilities, what came
under my observation.

My arrival here was — I may say it without vanity,
for I was a stranger to him—quite an event in the poor
missionary's lonely life; and the landing—for it did not

deserve the name of room—left vacant by the departure
of Father Arnoux, was placed at my disposal. I ask
pardon of the good, brave, and generous priests who have
aided, welcomed, and sheltered me through all my
wanderings, if I have spoken too plainly of their poverty
and privations of all kinds; if I have raised the curtain
which, perhaps, they would wish to keep drawn, for, I
repeat, they look not for recompense in this world; but
I have done it that the world may know that their life is
one of the hardest and most painful, and requires self-
sacrifice more than any other. Exposed to the influence
of pernicious climates, badly lodged, badly fed, far from
their families and from their country, often ill and dying
without help—such is the lot of these men.

The house of uncle Apait was at least as elegant and
well furnished as that of the humble priest at Brelum:
both had the bare ground for a floor, walls of bamboo
canes, and dried grass for thatch. The hut was divided
into four compartments, two being used by the missionaries, another by their servant, and the fourth served as a
chapel. This, like the others, was far from splendid, and
the whole house had been so undermined by the white
ants, that it seemed menaced with approaching ruin.

Speaking of the Annamite servants, I shall quote what
the Abbé Gagelin says about them, for I can testify to its
truth. "All sensibility," says he, "appears deadened
among them; they are very proud, however, and great
cheats. There is so little affection among them, that the
nearest relations never think of embracing; even a child,

Drawn by M. H. Rousseau, from a Photograph.

AMAZON OF THE KING'S FEMALE GUARDS.

returning to his parents after a ten years' absence, would
not think of such a thing. Among brothers and sisters
it would be considered almost a scandal. They will not
permit us missionaries to caress a child, not even a baby.
This coldness is not confined to their domestic relations;
under an ardent sky, which should warm the imagination,
they, in their stupid *sang froid*, will not tolerate in a
preacher the slightest movement or gesture." However,
to compensate for these defects, the abbé, who, even in
the opinion of several of the other missionaries, has been
guilty of great errors in his letters, might have added that,
at times, they are capable of acts of devotion and self-
sacrifice truly great and courageous.

The French missionaries in Cochin China must have
had many proofs of this, for, hunted as they are like wild
beasts, they could not long escape the vigilant eyes of the
mandarins, nor continue, in spite of the most terrible
persecutions, to reside in the country. It is death for
any one to be caught sheltering or assisting a priest;
but, notwithstanding, they and their goods are conveyed
in boats from Singapore, eluding all the spies set to watch
for them, and remain hidden for months and even years.
If an alarm is raised, in spite of the danger of discovery,
they are conveyed to another locality, where they find
new friends equally ready to peril their lives for them.
Missions are founded amongst the most savage tribes;
and in spite of the terrible reputation of this climate, in
spite of fevers, wild beasts, and love of home, the missionary has but to speak, and he is sure to find poor

Christians ready to follow him, often without fee or
reward.   In what country in the world, among what
civilized people of the West, can you find more than
this?

Intelligent, and with a desire for civilization, the only
difficulty is to know how to guide them.   From my own
experience and that of others, I believe the Annamite to
be lively, adroit, intelligent, and courageous; but obstinate, vindictive, a dissembler, a liar, and a thief; slow
to get into a passion, but terrible when he does so.   His
dirtiness surpasses anything I have ever seen, and his
food is abominably nasty.   Rotten fish and dog's flesh are
his favourite diet.

The tiger of Annam is terribly savage, and his strength
is equal to his ferocity.   Often, however, a couple of men
will go alone to attack one, armed merely with pikes.   As
soon as they see the animal, the more powerful or more
courageous of the two lowers his pike; the tiger hesitates
a moment, and sometimes, if not pressed by hunger, turns
and disappears with the rapidity of lightning; but at
other times he will make a spring at the hunter, when,
if the force of the leap do not carry him right over the
man's head, he falls upon the pike, which the hunter then
elevates by pressing the handle on the ground.   The
second hunter now comes forward, and in his turn pierces
him, and uniting their strength, they both hold him down
till he dies.   Occasionally the first man misses his aim,
and his pike breaks; then all is over for one, if not both.
The most common method of hunting the tiger has more

SCENE IN THE JUNGLE BETWEEN BATTAMBONG AND BANGKOK.

Drawn by M. Catenacci, from a Sketch by M. Mouhot.

actors engaged.   There is in every village some experienced man who leads the attack; and if any one has
been carried off by one of these animals, the tam-tam is
sounded to summon people from the neighbouring villages
to follow this leader after the creature.   As he always
sleeps near the spot where he has left the remains of
his repast, they are pretty sure of discovering his retreat.

When they have tracked the tiger to his lair, all the
hunters form a circle as large as their number will allow,
and sufficiently apart not to impede each other's move-
ments.   These preparations completed, the leader makes
sure that the animal has no outlet for escape.   Some of
the most daring then venture into the centre and cut
away the brushwood, during which operation they are
protected by others armed with pikes.   The tiger, pressed
on all sides, rolls his eyes, licks his paws in a convulsive
manner, as though preparing for combat, then, with a
frightful howl, he makes his spring.   Immediately every
pike is raised, and the animal falls pierced through and
through.   Accidents not infrequently happen, and many
are often severely hurt; but they have no choice but to
wage war against the tigers, which leave them no rest,
force the enclosures, and carry off domestic animals and
even men, not only from the roads and close vicinity of
the houses, but from the interiors of the buildings.   In
Annam, the fear inspired by the tigers, elephants, and
other wild animals, makes the people address them with
the greatest respect; they give them the title of "Grand-

father" or "Lord," fearing that they may be offended, and show resentment by attacking them.

During the three months I passed in Brelum and its environs, my two poor servants were almost constantly ill with fever. I think myself very fortunate to have preserved my health, for even in these forests I have not had a touch of this complaint. In the rainy season the atmosphere is dreadfully damp and oppressive; in the thickest wood, where the sun scarcely penetrates, you might fancy yourself in a stove, and with the slightest exercise you are in a bath of perspiration.

In July and August we experienced violent storms, which burst out every second or third day; but in September and October it rained without intermission. At the beginning of November, after a change of wind, we had some refreshing nights, which made the thermometer fall to 12° centigrade. From noon to three o'clock there was little variation in the temperature.

Having paid visits to all the villages in the neighbourhood, and been visited in return by many of the inhabitants, I announced to my two excellent friends the missionaries that I must shortly leave them, and fixed my departure for the 29th November, meaning to return to Pinhalú and Udong, and from thence to ascend the Mekon as far as the great lake Touli-Sap.

CHAPTER XI.

ON the 29th I took leave of my amiable fellow-country-
man and friend, M. Arnoux, to, I may venture to affirm,
our mutual regret, and set off, accompanied by Father
Guilloux, who had some business at Pinhalú. They both
wished me to remain with them until Cochin China was
open, and I could travel through the country in safety :
I should have liked to do so, could I have foreseen an
approaching termination of the war; but in the then state
of affairs that was impossible.

As far as Pump-Ka-Daye, the first village we came to
after leaving Brelum, I had the society and aid of the missionaries, and of the old chief of the Stiêns, who furnished
me with three waggons for my baggage, while Phrai and
M. Guilloux's Annamite attendants took charge of my
boxes of insects, which, if placed among my other goods,
would have been injured by the jolting.

The rains had ceased for the last three weeks, and I
was agreeably surprised at the improvement in the state

of the country since August. The paths were dry, and we had no longer to flounder through dirty marshes, nor suffer from the wet nights which we formerly found so unpleasant. When we reached the station where we were to pass the first night, our servants lighted a fire to cook their rice, as well as scare away the wild beasts; but, notwithstanding this, we remarked that our oxen, dogs, and monkey showed signs of great fear, and, almost immediately afterwards, we heard a roaring like that of a lion. We seized our guns, which were loaded, and waited in readiness.

Fresh roarings, proceeding from a very short distance off, completed the terror of our animals; and we ourselves could not help feeling uneasy. I proposed to go and meet the enemy, which was agreed to, and we accordingly plunged into that part of the forest whence the sound came. Although familiar with these terrible creatures, we felt far from comfortable; but before long we came upon recent tracks which were quite unmistakeable, and soon, in a small clearing in the forest, perceived nine elephants, the leader being a male of enormous size, standing right in front of us.

On our approach he set up a roar more frightful than ever, and the whole herd advanced slowly towards us. We remained in a stooping position, half hidden behind the trees, which were too tall for us to climb. I was in the act of taking aim at the forehead of the leader, the only vulnerable part, but an Annamite who stood beside me, and who was an old hunter, knocked up my rifle,

Drawn by M. Catenacci, from a Sketch by M. Mouhot

HALT OF THE CARAVAN IN THE JUNGLE BETWEEN BATTAMBONG AND BANGKOK.

and begged me not to fire; "for," said he, "if you kill
or wound one of the elephants we are lost; and even if we
should succeed in escaping, the oxen, the waggons, and all
their contents would be overwhelmed by the fury of these
animals. If there were but two or three, we might hope
to kill them; but nine, of whom five are very large, are
too many; and it will be more prudent to retreat." At
this moment, Father Guilloux, who had not much confidence in his powers of locomotion, fired his gun in the air
to frighten the elephants; and this plan fortunately succeeded: the herd stopped in astonishment for an instant,
then turned round, and marched into the forest.

When we reached Pemptiélan we stopped at the house
of the mandarin, whose authority extends over the neighbouring district, and, contrary to the usual custom, he
offered us hospitality under his own roof. Scarcely, however, were we installed when he came to me and asked
for the best of my guns, and, on my declining to part
with it, he begged for something else, intimating that
we should have begun by offering a present. Thereupon
I gave him a suit of European clothes, a powder-flask and
some powder, a hunting-knife, and some other small articles.
In return he presented me with an ivory trumpet, and
placed at my service two elephants to enable me to continue my route more comfortably: he likewise sent off
our people with a letter to the chiefs of the Srokkhner.

We resumed our journey on the following day, the
Abbé on one elephant, reading his breviary, and I upon
another, both of us greatly enjoying the beauty of the

landscape. Thus we traversed the beautiful plains, which, when I formerly travelled this road, were inhabited by the poor Thiâmes; but now, in place of rich harvest, I was astonished to find nothing but large trees: the villages were abandoned, and the houses and enclosures in ruins. It appeared that the mandarin of Pemptiélan, executing or exceeding the orders of his master the king of Cambodia, had kept these unfortunate people in such a state of slavery and oppression that they had even been deprived of their fishing and agricultural implements, and, being left without money or resources, experienced such frightful poverty that many of them died of hunger.

The poor wretches, to the number of several thousands, and under the conduct of a chief on whose head a price had been set, and who had secretly returned from Annam, rose in revolt. Those from Penom-Peuh went to Udong to protect their brethren in that place in their flight; and when all were united in one body, they descended the river, and passed into Cochin China. Orders were issued by the king to arrest their departure, but no one remained to execute them ; for the whole Cambodian population, with the mandarins at their head, had fled into the forests at the first news of the rising.

Besides the interest inspired by the misfortunes of these poor people, their conduct, when all fled before them, and left Udong, Pinhalú, and Penom-Peuh defenceless, was so noble as greatly to increase this feeling. " We have no enmity against the people," said they, " if they will but let us pass and respect our property ; but we

will put to death whoever opposes our flight." And, in
fact, they never touched one of the large boats which
were moored near the market, and unguarded, but took
to the river in their narrow and miserable pirogues.

In passing opposite the island of Ko-Sutin we stopped
to see Father Cordier. The good missionary was in a sad
state: his malady had got worse; and his debility was
such that he could scarcely drag himself from his bed to
a chair. He had no food but rice and dried fish; and the
only persons to care for him, and wait upon him, were
two children of ten years old. We begged him to accompany us to Pinhalú, but he declined, on account of
his weakness. "All I regret," said he, "is, that I shall
see my poor parents no more; but for that, I should await
death calmly, and almost with joy." All our solicitations
that he would go with us were unavailing; and we were
forced to pursue our journey, very sad at leaving him in
so painful a position, and at our inability to give him any
relief.

On the 21st December we at last reached Pinhalú.

Penom-Peuh is about 103° 3' 50" long. of Paris, and
11° 37' 30" north lat. It is the great market of Cambodia, and only two or three leagues from the southern
frontier of Cochin China: it is situated at the confluence
of the Mekon with its tributary: from this point the river
flows first north-east, and then north-west, as far as China
and the mountains of Thibet. The arm, which has no
name, but which, to distinguish it, it might be well to call
Mé-Sap, from the name of the lake Touli-Sap, flows from

its source south-east to the point of junction. About 12° 25′ north lat. commences the great lake, which stretches as far as 13° 53′. In shape it might be compared to a violin. The whole space between it and the Mekon is a vast plain; while on the opposite side are the great chains of Poursat and its ramifications.

The entrance to the great lake of Cambodia is grand and beautiful. The river becomes wider and wider, until at last it is four or five miles in breadth; and then you enter the immense sheet of water called Touli-Sap, as large and full of motion as a sea. It is more than 120 miles long, and must be at least 400 in circumference.

The shore is low, and thickly covered with trees, which are half submerged; and in the distance is visible an extensive range of mountains whose highest peaks seem lost in the clouds. The waves glitter in the broad sunshine with a brilliancy which the eye can scarcely support, and, in many parts of the lake, nothing is visible all around but water. In the centre is planted a tall mast, indicating the boundary between the kingdoms of Siam and Cambodia. Before crossing the lake it may, perhaps, be as well to say what remains to be told respecting the latter country.

The present state of Cambodia is deplorable, and its future menacing.* Formerly, however, it was a powerful

---

* This prediction is already in part fulfilled by an insurrection in favour of the young prince, the king's brother, shortly after the departure of M. Mouhot. See the letter of M. Silvestre, 4th Jan. 1862.

Drawn by M. Thérond, from a Sketch by M. Mouhot

TOWER AT BANOME, NEAR BATTAMBONG.

and populous country, as is testified by the splendid ruins
which are to be met with in the provinces of Battambong and Ongcor, and which I intend visiting; but at
present the population is excessively reduced by the incessant wars carried on against neighbouring states. I do
not think that the country now contains above a million
of inhabitants, and, according to the last census, the
number of free men fit to carry arms is returned at 30,000,
the slaves, as in Siam, not being liable to serve in the
army any more than to pay taxes. Besides a number of
Chinese, relatively great, there are many Malays, who
have been settled in the country for centuries, and a
floating population of Annamites, amounting to two or
three thousand. As the calculations taken include only
the males fit for active service, no exact figures can be
furnished by the authorities.

European conquest, abolition of slavery, wise and pro-
tecting laws, and experience, fidelity, and scrupulous
rectitude in those who administer them, would alone effect
the regeneration of this state. It lies near to Cochin
China, the subjection of which France is now aiming at,
and in which she will doubtless succeed: under her sway
it will become a land of plenty. I wish her to possess
this land, which would add a magnificent jewel to her
crown; but it is also my earnest desire that she may
make a judicious choice of governors, and that the name of
France, my dear and beautiful country, may be loved,
respected, and honoured in the extreme East, as it should
be everywhere.

The chief productions of Cambodia are tobacco, pepper, ginger, sugar, gamboge, coffee, silk, and cotton. The latter important article of commerce thrives here admirably; and as, according to report, America is menaced with civil war, it is a question whether we can henceforth calculate on that country for the supply it has hitherto furnished. If that supply were even partially to fail, and thousands of workmen to be in consequence thrown out of employment, what a vast field might be opened on the banks of the Mekon and of Touli-Sap for European activity, industry, and capital!

England, that great nation for colonies, could soon make of Lower Cochin China and Cambodia a vast cotton plantation; and there is no doubt that, if she set about it in earnest, with her Australian, East and West Indian, and New Zealand possessions, she might soon secure to herself the monopoly, which America now has, of this precious article : we should in that case be compelled to buy from her. Why should we not be our own purveyors? The island of Ko-Sutin alone, in which the lands belonging to the crown are let to the cotton-planters in lots for one pound per lot, may be adduced in order to give an idea of the profits realized by the cultivation of this plant. Each lot affords an income of more than 1200 francs.

The forests situated on the higher grounds abound with justly-celebrated timber, as also trees yielding resins and gums much esteemed in commerce, likewise the eagle-wood and several species of dye-woods.

The mountains contain gold, argentiferous lead, zinc,

copper, and iron, the last two in some abundance. One
is astonished to find these fertile lands furnish so little for
exportation ; but the sovereigns and mandarins enrich
themselves by spoliation and extortion, and every abuse
which can ruin a country and retard its progress. If
these dominions were ruled wisely and carefully, with
probity, and with a regard to the interests of the working
classes, the whole aspect of affairs would be changed.

The taxes now weigh solely on the cultivator and pro-
ducer : the more he raises, the more he has to pay : disposed, therefore, to indolence by the influence of the
climate, he has little inducement to combat this vice.
The beautiful cardamom of Poursat, much sought after by
the Chinese, who pay very highly for it, is entirely mono-
polized by the king and his ministers ; and it is nearly
the same with every valuable product.

CHAPTER XII.

PRELIMINARY REMARKS.

NOKHOR, or Ongcor, was the capital of the ancient kingdom of Cambodia, or Khmer, formerly so famous among the great states of Indo-China, that almost the only tradition preserved in the country mentions that empire as having had twenty kings who paid tribute to it, as having kept up an army of five or six million soldiers, and that the buildings of the royal treasury occupied a space of more than 300 miles.*

In the province still bearing the name of Ongcor, which is situated eastward of the great lake Touli-Sap, towards the 14th degree of north lat., and 104° long. east of Greenwich, there are, on the banks of the Mekon, and in the ancient kingdom of Tsiampois (Cochin-China), ruins of such grandeur, remains of structures which must have been raised at such an immense cost of labour, that, at the first view, one is filled with profound admiration, and cannot but ask what has become of this powerful race,

---

* Sic in orig.—*Tr.*

The material originally positioned here is too large for reproduction in this reissue. A PDF can be downloaded from the web address given on page iv of this book, by clicking on 'Resources Available'.

so civilised, so enlightened, the authors of these gigantic works?

One of these temples—a rival to that of Solomon, and erected by some ancient Michael Angelo—might take an honourable place beside our most beautiful buildings. It is grander than anything left to us by Greece or Rome, and presents a sad contrast to the state of barbarism in which the nation is now plunged.

Unluckily the scourge of war, aided by time, the great destroyer, who respects nothing, and perhaps also by earthquakes, has fallen heavily on the greater part of the other monuments; and the work of destruction and decay continues among those which still remain standing, imposing and majestic, amidst the masses of ruins all around.

One seeks in vain for any historical souvenirs of the many kings who must have succeeded one another on the throne of the powerful empire of Maha-Nocor-Khmer. There exists a tradition of a leprous king, to whom is attributed the commencement of the great temple, but all else is totally forgotten. The inscriptions, with which some of the columns are covered, are illegible; and, if you interrogate the Cambodians as to the founders of Ongcor-Wat, you invariably receive one of these four replies: " It is the work of Pra-Eun, the king of the angels; " " It is the work of the giants; " " It was built by the leprous king; " or else, " It made itself."

The work of giants! The expression would be very just, if used figuratively, in speaking of these prodigious works, of which no one who has not seen them can form any adequate idea; and in the construction of which patience, strength, and genius appear to have done their utmost in order to leave to future generations proofs of their power and civilisation.

It is remarkable that none of these monuments were intended for habitations; all were temples of Buddhism. The statues and bas-reliefs, however, curiously enough, represent entirely secular. subjects—monarchs surrounded by their wives, their heads and arms loaded with ornaments such as bracelets and necklaces, the body being covered with a narrow *langouti*. On a sort of esplanade is a statue, said to be that of the leprous king. It is a little above the middle height, and the prince is seated in a noble and dignified attitude. The head, particularly, is a *chef-d'œuvre*, the features perfectly regular, and possessing a manly beauty of a description seen now in very rare instances, and only amongst Cambodians of unmixed race, living in seclusion at the foot of the mountains, where the unhealthiness of the climate condemns them to a solitary existence; or among the savage mountaineers who occupy the border country separating Siam and Cambodia from the kingdom of Annam.

This place was probably chosen for the capital on account of its central position. It is situated fifteen miles from the great lake, in an arid and sandy plain, although the banks of the river would appear to have been a preferable site, more fertile, and offering greater facilities for communication.

Although making no pretension whatever either to

Drawn by M. Thérond, from a Sketch by M. Mouhot

STATUE OF THE LEPROUS KING.

architectural or archæological acquirements, I will endeavour to describe what I saw, for the benefit of others interested in these sciences, and, as well as I can, to draw the attention of Eastern *savans* to a new scene. I shall

commence with the temple of Ongcor, the most beautiful and best preserved of all the remains, and which is
also the first which presents itself to the eye of the traveller, making him forget all the fatigues of the journey,
filling him with admiration and delight, such as would
be experienced on finding a verdant oasis in the sandy
desert. Suddenly, and as if by enchantment, he seems to
be transported from barbarism to civilisation, from profound darkness to light.

But, ere I proceed with my description, I must express
my gratitude to the excellent missionary of Battambong,
the Abbé E. Silvestre, who, with exceeding courtesy and
indefatigable energy, accompanied me everywhere, guided
me through the thick forest which covers a portion of
the site of the original building, and by whose assistance
I was enabled to accomplish so much in a limited time.

THE TEMPLE OF ONGCOR.

Before arriving at Ongcor from Battambong, having
previously crossed the great lake from the mouth of either
of the currents which traverse both those localities, you
come upon a stream, which, in the dry season, you ascend
for a couple of miles, and reach a spot where it becomes
somewhat larger, forming a small natural basin, which
serves the purpose of a kind of harbour. From this place
a raised causeway, still passable at the present day, and
extending as far as the limit which the waters attain at
the period of the inundations, that is to say, over a space
of three miles, leads to New Ongcor, an insignificant little

PRINCIPAL ENTRANCE OF THE GREAT TEMPLE OF ONGCOR WAT.

Drawn by M. Guiaud, from a Sketch by M. Mouhot.

town, the capital of the province, and situated fifteen
miles to the N.N.W. of the shores of the lake.

If, starting from this point, you follow for about a
couple of hours in the same direction a dusty sandy
path passing through a dense forest of stunted trees; and
having also frequently crossed the river, which is exceedingly sinuous in its course, you will arrive at an esplanade
about 9 metres wide by 27 long, parallel to the building.
At each angle, at the extremity of the two longer sides,
are two enormous lions, sculptured out of the rock, and
forming, with the pedestals, only a single block. Four
large flights of steps lead to the platform.

From the north staircase, which faces the principal
entrance, you skirt, in order to reach the latter, a causeway 230 metres in length by 9 in width, covered or paved
with large slabs of stone, and supported by walls of great
thickness. This causeway crosses a ditch 220 metres
wide, which surrounds the building; the revetment,
3 metres high by 1 metre thick, is formed of ferru-
ginous stone, with the exception of the top row, which is
of freestone, each block being of the same thickness as the
wall.

Principal Entrance.—The edifice forms a long gallery
with a central tower, and two others, of rather less alti
tude, about 30 metres distant from the former. The
portico of each tower is formed of four projecting columns,
with a staircase. At each extremity are similar porticoes,
beyond which, but immediately contiguous thereto, is a
high door or gateway, on the same level, which serves for

the passage of vehicles. From constant use the wheels have worn two deep ruts in the massive flagstones with which the ground is paved.

Upon the west side the gallery is supported by two rows of square columns; on the east, blank windows have been let into the wall, with stone railings or balconies of twisted columns 14 centimetres in diameter. The whole of this side, within one metre of the ground, and half a metre of the cornice, is covered with sculptures executed with marvellously artistic skill.

The roof—and in this respect it resembles all the other buildings—is a double one, constructed externally of sculptured stone, the blocks in the interior being plain; they were formerly hidden by a ceiling, also sculptured, of which some remains may still be remarked. The edifice divides the wall into two equal parts; upon the other sides, and facing the monument, are three pavilions, 33 metres in length.

This imposing colonnade, which, from its great length and beautiful proportions, attracts the attention from a distance, forms a fitting entrance to the great monument.

The Temple.—Commencing from the building which forms the principal entrance, is a second causeway, 9 metres wide by 342 metres in length; it is raised 1 metre from the level of the ground. It is covered with huge blocks of stone, carefully joined together throughout its entire length, and is surrounded by a balustrade, partially in ruins, about 10 centimetres high, composed of long stones, with bevelled edges, very massive, and covered

TEMPLE OF ONGCOR WAT, NORTH SIDE.

Drawn by M. Guiaud, from a Sketch by M. Mouhot.

with sculptures. On each side are six platforms of earth, ascended by several steps, upon each of which is a serpent with seven heads, some erect, others thrown back.

In the centre of the causeway are two elegant pavilions, one on each side, having at each extremity a portico 33 metres 66 centimetres in length. At the end of the. causeway, and at the foot of the terrace, are, on each side of the latter, two ponds or sheets of water. A balustrade, like that of the causeway, and resting like it upon a sculptured basement, springs from the foot of the terrace, and runs all round the monument. At certain intervals there are large staircases of several steps each.

The Terrace.—The terrace is 2 metres 30 centimetres in height, and is surrounded by 112 fluted columns, surmounted by capitals, formed in each case of one single block of stone. The basement, like that of the whole building, is ornamented with very beautiful sculptured cornices, varied in style, and entirely covered with delicate carvings representing roses and arabesques, worked with the chisel, with a taste and skill equally wonderful.

This terrace forms a cross, each arm of which is 122 metres in length, and 12 metres 16 centimetres wide. There are three flights of steps, upon each of which are four lions reclining upon their pedestals.

The Portico.—This is 6 metres in length, and is supported by six columns, four of which are detached from the monument.

The temple is formed of three distinct parts raised in the form of terraces one above the other.

The Galleries.—The galleries form a rectangle, the façade of which is 180 metres in length; the sides 216 metres 16 centimetres by 4 metres 16 centimetres.

The vaulted ceilings of the galleries are raised 6 metres from the ground; those of the second roof are 4 metres 30 centimetres high. The two roofs are supported by a double row of columns, the first being 3 metres 18 centimetres and the second 2 metres 25 centimetres high by 48 centimetres broad. The columns are square, and, like all other buildings in the province, are formed of single blocks.

There are five staircases on the west side, the same number on the east, and three on each of the remaining sides.

The basement is 3 metres 90 centimetres in height, the length externally forming a terrace of 1 metre 57 centimetres.

Each portico is composed of three roofs raised one above the other, which contribute materially to give to the architecture of these long galleries a monumental appearance, producing a singularly beautiful effect.

The opposite side of the wall to the double colonnade is, from the lowest row of cornices to one metre above its base, covered inside with bas-reliefs, having externally blank windows with balustrades.

There are two rows of cornices, the first part immediately above the columns; and the space, to the extent of nearly one metre, which lies between them, is filled up by roses and other sculptured designs.

CARVINGS OF ARMS UTENSILS, AND ORNAMENTS, AT ONGCOR-WAT

The bas-reliefs represent the combat of the king of the apes with the king of the angels:* in the centre is the king of the angels, drawn by two griffins; he has seven heads and twenty arms, with a sabre in each hand. Some of the chiefs are seated in cars drawn by fabulous animals, while others are mounted on elephants. The soldiers are armed with bows, javelins, or sabres, but the apes have generally no weapons except their formidable claws: a few of them have clubs, sabres, or branches of trees.

Peristyle No. 1.—Here is represented the march of warriors mounted on birds, horses, tigers, and fabulous animals; the horses of the chiefs are led by the bridle. On the right the soldiers are advancing towards the scene of combat in the centre; but here there are no fantastic animals.

Peristyle No. 2.—The bas-reliefs of this peristyle represent the combat between the king of the apes and the king of the angels, and the death of the former. Close by is a boat filled with rowers, all with long beards, and some of them attired in the Chinese fashion: the group is admirable for the natural positions and for the expression given to the faces. A cock-fight, and women at play with their children, are also represented. It is in these bas-reliefs that the highest degree of skill is shown.

---

* These sculptures probably represent the story of the Hindu Ramdyana, of great reputation among Buddhist nations. The *angel* is Ramana, Tyrant of Ceylon; and the King of the Monkeys, Hanuman Rama's General.

Other subjects follow, the meaning of which I could not discover.

On the south side, to the left hand, is a military procession—bodies of soldiers headed by chiefs, some mounted on elephants, others on horseback, and each corps carrying different arms, lances, halberds, javelins, sabres, and bows. On the right are two series, one representing the Hindu Paradise Swarga, the other the Hindu infernal regions Naralma. A crowd of persons are entering Paradise, and are received in palanquins: they have with them banners, fans, parasols, and boxes for holding betel, without which even Paradise would not be perfect happiness to a Cambodian.

A triumphal march. Paradise.—The elect seated on a magnificent dais, surrounded by a great number of women, with caskets and fans in their hands, while the men are holding flowers and have children on their knees. These appear to be all the joys of Paradise.

The punishments of the infernal regions, on the contrary, are varied and numerous; and while the elect, who are enjoying themselves in Paradise, are all fat and plump, the poor condemned beings are so lean that their bones show through their skin, and the expression of their faces is pitiful and full of a most comic seriousness. Some are being pounded in mortars, while others hold them by the feet and hands; some are being sawn asunder; others are led along, like buffaloes, with ropes through their noses. In other places the *comphubal* (executioners) are cutting men to pieces with sabres; while a crowd of poor wretches are being transfixed by the tusks of elephants, or on the horns of rhinoceros. Fabulous animals are busy devouring some; others are in irons, and have had their eyes put out.

In the centre sits the judge with his ministers, all sabre in hand, and the guilty are dragged before them by the hair or feet. In the distance is visible a furnace and another crowd of people under punishment, being tortured in divers ways—impaled, roasted on spits, tied to trees and pierced with arrows, suspended with heavy weights attached to their hands and feet, devoured by dogs or vultures, or crucified with nails through their bodies.

These bas-reliefs are perfect; the rest are inferior in workmanship and expression.

On the east side, a number of men, divided into two equal groups, are represented as attempting to drag in contrary directions the great serpent or dragon with seven heads, while, in the centre, an angel stands looking on. Many angels are seen floating in the sky above, while fishes, aquatic animals, and marine monsters swim about in a sea visible beneath. The angel is seated on the celebrated mountain of Thibet, Pra Soumer, and in different places angels with several heads give assistance to those pulling the serpent. The king of the apes, Sdach Soa, appears also here.

To the right is a military procession and a combat, the chiefs being mounted on elephants, unicorns, griffins, eagles with peacocks' tails, and other fantastic animals, while winged dragons draw the cars.

On the northern side is portrayed a combat, and procession, with drums, flutes, trumpets, tam-tams, and organs said to be Chinese; a king, mounted on the shoulders of a hideous giant, who holds in each hand by the foot a fighting giant. All the chiefs take part in the combat, standing, some on tigers, others in cars.

Near the central peristyle is a figure of the king, with a long beard; on each side are courtiers with clasped hands.

To the right appears a military procession, a combat, griffins, eagles with peacocks' tails, a dragon with seven heads and a tower on his back—the king letting fly an arrow, standing on the back of a giant with tail, claws, and beak.

Second Story.—The first gallery on the west side is connected with the second by two other smaller galleries, 40 metres long, and which are themselves connected by two colonnades in the form of a cross, and supporting two vaulted roofs.

Four rows of square columns, each hewn out of a single block of stone, those in the inside row being 4 metres 14 centimetres high and 45 centimetres thick; those on the outside being 3 metres 10 centimetres high, and rather smaller at the top than at the base. The little gallery on the right is filled with statues representing persons in the act of worshipping idols, some of these being of wood, others of stone. Many of the statues are 4 metres in height, and the greater number of them must be of great age, to judge from their state of dilapidation,

in spite of the hardness of the stone. In the centre is
a statue of the famous leprous king, and by his side, in a
posture of adoration, are two statues of priests, with faces

Drawn by M. Thérond, from a Sketch by M. Mouhot.

PAVILION IN THE INTERIOR OF THE TEMPLE OF ONGCOR-WAT.

full of expression. These are real chefs-d'œuvre. At no
great distance is a small statue of his queen.

Here are found two pavilions of extremely elegant architecture, with porticoes and staircases at each end.

There is a second gallery, with four towers at each end and three porticoes and staircases on each side. This gallery is raised on a base 5 metres 10 centimetres high, the ledge of which forms a terrace 74 centimetres broad.

There are neither columns nor bas-reliefs here, but the walls have imitation windows with twisted bars; the gallery is half dark, receiving very little light except through the doors. There are idols, both of stone and bronze, on pedestals, with their hands held out to receive gifts from their worshippers.

Central part.—A raised terrace leads to the foot of the great staircase, and forms a cross, the arms of which lead to two small pavilions with four porticoes and staircases. The base of this part is admirably executed, both as to general effect and in detail. There are twelve staircases, the four in the middle being 6 metres wide, and having 39 steps.

The building forms a square, each side of which is 56 metres 60 centimetres, and at each angle is a tower. A central tower, larger and higher, is connected with the lateral galleries by colonnades covered, like the galleries, with a double roof; and both galleries and colonnades are supported on a base one metre from the floor of the interior courts.

Opposite each of the twelve staircases is a small portico with four colums, 4 metres 50 centimetres high,

Vol. I. p. 208.

CENTRAL PORTICO OF THE GREAT TEMPLE OF ONGCOR WAT.

Drawn by M. Thérond, from a Sketch by M. Mouhot.

The material originally positioned here is too large for reproduction in this reissue. A PDF can be downloaded from the web address given on page iv of this book, by clicking on 'Resources Available'.

and 47 centimetres in diameter. Windows, similar in
form and dimension to those of the other galleries, are
on each side, and have twisted bars carved in stone.

In front of each colonnade, with an entrance in the
tower, is a dark and narrow chapel, to which there is an
ascent of eight steps. These four chapels do not com-
municate with each other. Each contains an idol 4 metres
in height, sculptured in the solid wall, at whose feet is
another nearly 2 metres long, representing Samanakodom
sleeping. The central tower is 33 metres high from the
pavement of the gallery, and 50 from the basement of the
building.

What strikes the observer with not less admiration than
the grandeur, regularity, and beauty of these majestic
buildings, is the immense size and prodigious number of
the blocks of stone of which they are constructed. In this
temple alone are as many as 1532 columns. What means
of transport, what a multitude of workmen, must this have
required, seeing that the mountain out of which the stone
was hewn is thirty miles distant! In each block are to
be seen holes $2\frac{1}{2}$ centimetres in diameter and 3 in depth,
the number varying with the size of the blocks; but the
columns and the sculptured portions of the building bear
no traces of them. According to a Cambodian legend,
these are the prints of the fingers of a giant, who, after
kneading an enormous quantity of clay, had cut it into
blocks and carved it, turning it into a hard and, at the
same time, light stone by pouring over it some marvellous
liquid.

All the mouldings, sculptures, and bas-reliefs appear to have been executed after the erection of the building. The stones are everywhere fitted together in so perfect a manner that you can scarcely see where are the joinings ; there is neither sign of mortar nor mark of the chisel, the surface being as polished as marble. Was this incomparable edifice the work of a single genius, who conceived the idea, and watched over the execution of it ? One is tempted to think so ; for no part of it is deficient, faulty, or inconsistent. To what epoch does it owe its origin ? As before remarked, neither tradition nor written inscriptions furnish any certain information upon this point ; or rather, I should say, these latter are as a sealed book for want of an interpreter ; and they may, perchance, throw light on the subject when some European savant shall succeed in deciphering them.

RUINS IN THE PROVINCE OF ONGCOR.   MOUNT BAKHENG.

A temple, about 100 metres in height, built of limestone has been erected on the top of Mount Bakhêng, which is situated two miles and a half north of Ongcor-Wat, on the road leading to the town. At the foot of the mountain are to be seen, among the trees, two magnificent lions, 20 centimetres in height, and each formed, with the pedestals, out of a single block. Steps, partly destroyed, lead to the top of the mountain, whence is to be enjoyed a view so beautiful and extensive, that it is not surprising that these people, who have shown so

much taste in their buildings, should have chosen it for
a site.

On the one side you gaze upon the wooded plain and
the pyramidal temple of Ongcor, with its rich colonnades,
the mountain of Crome, which is beyond the new city,
the view losing itself in the waters of the great lake on
the horizon. On the opposite side stretches the long chain
of mountains whose quarries, they say, furnished the
beautiful stone used for the temples; and amidst thick
forests, which extend along the base, is a pretty, small
lake, which looks like a blue ribbon on a carpet of verdure. All this region is now as lonely and deserted as
formerly it must have been full of life and cheerfulness;
and the howling of wild animals, and the cries of a few
birds, alone disturb the solitude.

Sad fragility of human things! How many centuries
and thousands of generations have passed away, of which
history, probably, will never tell us anything: what riches
and treasures of art will remain for ever buried beneath
these ruins; how many distinguished men—artists, sovereigns, and warriors—whose names were worthy of immor-
tality, are now forgotten, laid to rest under the thick dust
which covers these tombs!

The whole summit of the mountain is covered with
a coating of lime, forming a vast smooth surface. At
regular intervals are four rows of deep holes, in some of
which still stand the columns that formerly supported
two roofs, and formed a gallery leading from the staircase
to the principal part of the building, and the transverse

branches of which were connected with four towers, built partly of stone, partly of brick. Judging from the details of the work, and the state of the stone, which in many places crumbles at a touch, this building belongs to a period much anterior to that of many of the other monuments. Art, like science, was then in its infancy; difficulties were surmounted, but not without great efforts of labour and intelligence; taste was of a grand description, but genius was not in proportion; in a word, the temple of Mount Bakhêng appears to have been the prelude to civilization, while that of Ongcor-Wat was probably its climax.

In the two towers, which are least dilapidated, and which the modern worshippers have covered with a thatched roof, the old one having fallen in, are large idols rudely fashioned, and bearing marks of great age. In one of the other towers is a large stone, the inscription on which is still visible; and on the exterior wall is carved the figure of a king with a long beard, the only portion of bas-relief remaining.

A wall surrounds the top of the mountain. Bakhêng has also its Phrâbat, but it is a facsimile of recent origin. The building is quadrangular, and composed of five stories, each 3 metres high. That at the base is 68 metres square. They form so many terraces, which serve as bases to seventy-two small but elegant pavilions; and they are enriched with mouldings, colonnades, and cornices, but no sculpture. The work is perfect; and from its good state of preservation would seem to be of a more recent date

than the towers.   It is evident that each of these little
pavilions formerly contained an idol.

Each side of the square has a staircase 2 metres wide,
with nine steps to each story, and lions on each terrace.
The centre of the terrace formed by the last story is only
a confused mass of ruins from the fallen towers.   Near
the staircase are two gigantic blocks of very fine stone,
as polished as marble, and shaped like pedestals for
statues.

END OF VOL. I.

LONDON: PRINTED BY W. CLOWES AND SONS, STAMFORD STREET,
AND CHARING CROSS.

Lightning Source UK Ltd.
Milton Keynes UK
UKOW02f1942010615

252702UK00001B/26/P